1979

CHARACTERISTICS OF LOCAL MEDIA AUDIENCES

Characteristics of local media audiences

RAY BROWN

 SAXON HOUSE

Published by
Saxon House, Teakfield Limited,
Westmead, Farnborough, Hampshire, England

 British Library Cataloguing in Publication Data

Brown, Ray
    Characteristics of local media audiences.
    1. Mass media   2. Radio audiences
    3. Newspaper reading
    I. Title
    301.16'2   P91

    ISBN 0-566-00218-3

ISBN   0 566 00218 3

Printed and bound by Ilfadrove Limited,
Barry, S. Glamorgan, S. Wales.

Contents *301.162 B932*

v

List of Tables

Preface

The research described in this report was financed by the British Broadcasting Corporation with subsidiary support from the Royal Commission on the Press. The Centre for Television Research has been the home of numerous projects since its foundation in 1966. During the last decade (and, in fact, during the period of the now defunct Granada Television Research Fellowship, which was first housed at Leeds University in 1959), the Centre for Television Research has concentrated especially upon exploration of mass media roles in serving the felt needs of audience members.

Since the late 1960s a revitalised approach to the study of mass communications has gained increasing recognition and influence. Sometimes termed a 'uses and gratifications' approach to mass communication research, the Leeds Centre has been in the forefront of its development in Britain.

Brian Emmett, Head of BBC Audience Research Department, being familiar with the Centre's activities, approached the Centre's Director of Research, Dr Jay G. Blumler, and suggested that a 'uses and gratifications' study of local radio might well provide both theoretical advancement and findings that would assist the Audience Research Department and local radio staff in their professional activities. As a consequence of this suggestion, and following discussions with the BBC Head of Local Radio, Michael Barton, the present investigation was officially started in May 1974.

Support from the Royal Commission on the Press allowed an expansion of the study to include an analysis of the uses and gratifications associated with the reading of local newspapers, the conversion of some interviews from self completion to interviewer administered and an increase in total sample size from 1,000 to 1,300.

Many people contributed to this study in many ways. Apart from those already mentioned, who provided invaluable advice and assistance, I should mention my family: Sue, James, Sally and Dem—they often carried me and always gave support. I would like to thank local radio personnel, the interviewers who asked my strange questions, and those members of the public who answered them. Others who earned my gratitude were: Charlotte Allen, Christine Bailey, Francis Golding, Flo Green, George Kent, May Kitching, Paul McQuail and Jane Steedman. When the going was really rough, and funds were low, Alison Ewbank of the Centre for Television Research gave more hours than either of us care to remember; together we tackled the more boring aspect of social science — converting several thousand answers into numbers. Without Alison this study would have fallen at the penultimate fence. Many people helped, but the opinions, methods and errors are my own.

During the period of this project, after a meaningful life devoted to others, my sister died a meaningless, random death. Although it is far from worthy of her, this book is dedicated to my sister Ivy.

Introduction

The aim of research is to modify an existing understanding — to make
it more secure or to undermine it, in either case, to shed light on its
underlying assumptions. The researcher attempts this by posing
questions, answering them, then, from a modified standpoint
reassessing the landscape. The resulting outlook always has one
common feature, which is an entire new crop of questions swathed in
morning mist, and, rising above them, one or two old questions that
the researcher has yet to answer. The truth may be that research does
not merely explore reality but, gradually, over the years, also creates
it — this by modifying our existing understanding.

Such an introductory paragraph reads as if written to discourage
readers from the expectation that Table 6.1, or even Tables 6.1 to
6.50, will give all the answers to questions that might be asked about
people's expectations of their local communications media. That was
my intention. Of course, the report contains some answers and will, I
hope, give insights and satisfaction to its readers. Whilst writing I have
particularly in mind the lay and professional local broadcaster. I want
to show him or her that the oddly labelled 'uses and gratifications'
theory of audiences is rather similar to the ideas about audiences that
shape the day to day activities of most enthusiastic local broadcasters.
'Uses and gratifications' are about audience members' feelings of
expectation and satisfaction as focused on familiar offerings. This
research attempted to identify and measure the most prevalent
feelings of this kind that bear on local radio, local newspapers and
regional TV programmes. It also attempted to identify and measure
the feelings people have about their localities, and to measure various
factors which influence those feelings. For example, how long had
they lived in the locality? How many of their friends and relations
lived around them? Finally, the research attempted to bring these,
and other areas of evidence together, to associate them in order to
give the broadcaster a somewhat clearer impression of the motives of
his audience and the dynamics that may underlie these. And although
he or she will be left with some confusion and doubts, at least some of
them will be new ones, and some of the old questions will have been
answered.

If any of my informal aims are to be met, it is essential that the
smiling reader who hovers around me in excited anticipation should

understand this report. To that end alone I have taken certain liberties: occasionally using dubious but simple statistical devices — and determinedly defining all but the most commonplace jargon. And, because decimal points sometimes confuse the point, I have, unless quite inappropriate, changed 27.8375, and its like, into 28. This practice, along with the use of percentages, sometimes leads to tables which present 102 per cent of, say, listeners — which is a fact of arithmetic to be lived with.

1 Background to the Study

1. LOCAL RADIO

In December 1966 the British Government issued a White Paper
concisely entitled *Broadcasting*. This document laid down the
guidelines for the development of a new system of local radio stations
around the country and authorised the British Broadcasting
Corporation to establish nine experimental stations. The first station,
Radio Brighton, began transmitting on 14 February 1968, others
quickly followed. Independent Local Radio (ILR), financed by
advertising revenue and overseen by the Independent Broadcasting
Authority, arrived in the early 1970s: first London Broadcasting,
then Capital Radio, both in October 1973, both stations located in,
and broadcasting to, Greater London. The United Kingdom now has
just short of forty local stations, half ILR, half BBC. Further
developments and expansion have been urged by a recent commission
on broadcasting chaired by Lord Annan.

Local radio has been a growth area in British broadcasting, but
little evidence exists as to how well it is serving its audience.
Admittedly the BBC publishes daily patronage figures, but these tell
us nothing about the quality of local broadcasting, nor audience
reactions to it. And although ILR stations provide impressive
'listening figures' (in order to sell 'space' to advertisers) these data are
simply more realistic versions of the BBC figures, again they tell us
nothing whatsoever about the experience of listening, its satisfactions,
or the role of local radio in community life. The emphasis of this
study is not on size of audience, rather I was concerned to investigate
the nature of the relationships that exist between members of the
public and their local media. The Government White Paper,
Broadcasting, emphasised that local radio should be 'produced as a
public service' — I wondered how the public were utilising this new
service.

2. USES AND GRATIFICATIONS RESEARCH

An increasing proportion of our society has paid out money, and devoted time, in order to achieve skills which seemingly allow the mind to drift, or to be wiped clean, for a limited period of time. Mindlessness achieved through meditation, or whatever, is a fairly difficult state to reach. And yet one of our most popular leisure activities — receiving mass communications — is frequently termed 'mindless'. This is an instance of sloppy language. When we refer to a mindless mistake, we more often mean that our mind was engaged on something other than the task at hand. And when we watch television, or listen to radio, few of us reach that mindless state that others might find with the guidance of a guru (be he the Guru Maharishi himself, or a local leisure class teacher). What does go on in our heads when we attend to media? Strangely, this question has been ignored by many mass communications researchers. Until quite recently they have favoured the question, 'What does the medium do to people?' rather than, 'What do people do with the medium?'.

It is an important distinction; the two questions have quite different ramifications and implications. 'Uses and gratifications', as the words suggest, is focused on what people do with media. They use a medium in characteristic ways, and they seek certain satisfactions or gratifications — in this context the two terms are more or less synonymous. 'Uses and gratifications' is a very commonsense approach. It fits with our own experience as audience members, and, more or less implicitly, it influences the aims of all but the most didactic of broadcasters. It is largely inconsistent with the assumption that a programme can have some mass and uniform effect upon its audience. Such a phenomenon is rare because we bring to the medium a vast, though all too easily transportable, complex of personal prejudices, expectations, experience and distractions. The audience member is an individual, and because of our distinctive natures, no two of us ever really receive the same programme. Little wonder that the study of mass media effects has sometimes helped to produce a confusion that feeds any of the prejudiced views so often expressed in debate, editorial, and letters column.

The uses and gratifications 'theory', 'approach', 'orientation', 'tradition' — call it what you will — has tended to pass through two distinct phases (though the insightful reader would be correct to assume that nothing is quite so simple as that). An initial formulation in the early 1940s encouraged research which gradually petered out in the 1950s. It was an armchair approach which virtually allowed the researcher to go to the pictures and then be opinionated. At its best, and this has rarely been bettered, the research entailed lengthy and sympathetic interviews with audience members or programme fans. But such activities were inconsistent with the number-crunching, computerised fashions which still dominate social science. Just to find out how people understood their favourite programme, what they got out of it, was not enough. It became necessary to measure the satisfactions and uses, to turn them into numbers that could be manipulated and then related to other 'variables'. The Leeds University Centre for Television Research was one of several academic institutions around the world which coincidentally began the process of quantifying 'uses and gratifications' in the late 1960s and early 1970s. To appreciate the breadth of this movement, and to sample its products, the reader is directed to *The Uses of Mass Communications,* edited by Jay G. Blumler and E. Katz (1974).

For the purpose of this report, it is only necessary at this stage to bear a few basic 'uses and gratifications' assumptions in mind, plus a first acquaintance with the techniques developed at Leeds. Our studies have been consistent with the earliest work, in as much as we have always emphasised the importance of audience experience, and extensive contact with appropriate members of the public is, in our opinion, an essential precursor to questionnaire design and survey — more of this later. At its most simple our technique is as follows:

> Discursive group discussions are conducted and audio-taped. Respondents are selected according to the focus of research, and they meet in homes which approximate their own. Tapes are analysed for specific statements concerning the uses of broadcast material (e.g. I often find that I talk about . . .) and satisfactions sought or attained (I must admit . . . always leaves me feeling better). These statements, plus others from earlier work, are tidied and put into a pre-formulated list, which allows informants to endorse them with some degree of agreement or recognition. Endorsements, usually on scales of three to five points, are coded as numbers and fed into a computer. The average scores of different groups can then be compared; also the relationships between particular items can be assessed and, probably, these items can be brought together into meaningful clusters or ideas (e.g. the present study shows such a cluster of satisfactions found in listening to local radio — a number of items are brought together which clearly suggest the idea of local radio as a friendly, personal medium).

Although our techniques are rarely more complex than suggested by the above outline, they are far more thorough than might be supposed. For instance, the questionnaire itself proceeds through several drafts, most of which are assessed and modified in the light of pilot surveys. Great care is also taken to ensure that the potential respondent fully understands the questions, is familiar with expressions used, and is not overloaded or bored. In effect the first tangible results of this approach are the questionnaire design and contents. The questionnaire taps actual experience, and it should not go beyond the respondent's range of experience. Every questionnaire will produce results — that is the curse of survey work — only careful preparation and piloting will ensure that the results are not inadequate from the word 'go'. There are other critical points, sample selection and the briefing of interviewers, for example, but regardless of how excellent any other feature of the work is, the whole edifice is only as good as the questionnaire. And results from surveys are really rather meaningless unless the reader is familiar with the questions that produced them. Even basic audience figures depend upon who asks what of whom; to appreciate the meaning of a set of figures it is more important to ask that simple question than to be versed in sophisticated statistics.

3. BBC AND THE CENTRE FOR TELEVISION RESEARCH

The Centre for Television Research is an academic institute which has housed many research projects over the years. Whilst it has never conducted 'commissioned' research, preferring to maintain control over the course and content of its studies, the Centre has always hoped that its work would be of value to broadcasters. And the Centre has never shunned financial assistance from industry, so long as the money was not tied up in strings; in fact considerable support for one project or another has been provided by, amongst others, the BBC, the IBA, the Department of Education and Science and a large advertising agency.[1] The Head of Audience Research, BBC, was, of course, aware of the Centre's position *vis-a-vis* financial support, and also intimately familiar with the output of communications researchers both at home and abroad. His proposition, that the BBC ARD should finance a small scale uses and gratifications investigation of local radio, was favourably received. It was also agreed that whilst the Centre was to be given 'academic freedom', the BBC would be entitled to comment on report drafts and to be consulted over the timing of any publications. Furthermore, the Centre agreed to involve the BBC ARD in the selection of geographical areas within which the research would be conducted. It was assumed, correctly, that no major conflict of interests would occur, and although the BBC emphasised, and realised, a desire to include two nominated cities in the study, their requests could not be regarded as inordinate, nor as a source of strain upon the Centre's academic freedom.

It can be assumed, then, that the BBC has had some say in this work, both directly through consultation with the Heads of ARD and Local Radio, and also, as will become apparent, indirectly through the willing cooperation of several BBC Local Radio Station Managers who gave up their scarce time in order to familiarise the Centre with their philosophies, concerns, beliefs and practices.

NOTES

[1] Of course, other sources of research funding have supported Centre work as well, including the Social Science Research Council, the Leverhulme Trust and the Rowntree Social Services Trust.

2 Defining the Research Problem

Having agreed to undertake a study, the Centre was faced with the general question of what to do. From the very beginning all parties agreed that the research should be representative of the 'Leeds' approach to the study of audience gratifications. This narrowed down the options; by accepting the traditional survey approach with an audience focus there was no question of, for instance, detailed studies of broadcast material, 'action research', or analyses of station procedure. And time constraints made any worthwhile 'panel operation' (in which the informant is approached for interview on two or more occasions) inappropriate. In fact, even before the first draft proposal was envisaged, an overall time structure was clear. Past experience suggested that a two year period would break down into one year of background, desk research, qualitative work, piloting and general administration and preparation. Fieldwork itself should be completed in as brief a period as possible — in order to minimise the effects of extraneous variables beyond our control: acts of God, government, and so on. This would leave slightly less than a year for data coding, analysis and preliminary write-up. A rather tight time budget, but, other things being equal, and with luck on our side, one which could be met.

The central problem at this stage was related to the notion of uses and gratifications. For several reasons local media in general, and local radio in particular, seemed to be an excellent focus for application of this approach. But in the early days it was necessary to achieve some fairly clear ideas about how the approach could be adapted to local communications: what exactly are local communications in uses and gratification terms? The outcome of intensive discussions involving Centre staff experienced in gratification research was a brief and recognisably imperfect working document written in the form of a research proposal. However imperfect, the paper contained, along with methodological formalities, an important theoretical statement, namely, the introduction of the term, 'local communications requirements'. The point is that two quite different applications of gratification theory could be found. We could view local media as a special sub-set of national media, serving essentially the same functions, providing similar satisfactions. Or maybe local media are different; perhaps they provide satisfactions that are dissimilar and specific to themselves. Clearly there would be high overlap between local and national media in terms of the audience satisfactions for which they catered, but, equally clearly, content and organisation were dissimilar. Whilst a sound argument could be made that the 'local flavour' did no more than facilitate listening, making it easier for certain people to gain media-based gratifications from local than from national sources (and, of course, inhibit patronage, making it difficult for other individuals to find satisfaction in the local medium with its regional accents and civic politics), it seemed wiser at that stage to accept the concept of 'local communications requirements' as a working premise. And, in order to do that, a further structuring of the research was necessary; it became apparent that we must study local radio in the context of other local media.

On another front it has to be admitted that our first hand experience of radio research was rather limited, as indeed, was our first hand experience of local radio itself. In order to compensate for this, and as a means of ensuring that our work was relevant to the producers of local radio, another element was built into the study. This, to be undertaken as early as possible, was to involve Centre staff in visits to stations and interviews with personnel in order to become familiar with prevailing philosophies and practices. A by-product would be that we might be aided in arriving at a number of stations, or cities, most suited for the study. After further consultations with the BBC it was decided that the grant would become effective from June 1974, and the writer was designated principal researcher.

3 Overview of the Investigation's Structure and Content

Launching, maintaining and completing a research project of this nature is a fairly complex operation, especially in a university setting where few service departments are available, and the individual researcher is responsible for everything — payments, bookings, documentation, computer work and so on. The present project was further strained when inflation bit deeply into its budget, and certain jobs normally relying on cottage industry, such as converting the 1,300 questionnaires into sequences of numbers, had to be undertaken by already stretched Centre staff. However, the rough time schedule outlined above was observed.

An event which had some influence upon the project, both in terms of its scope and content, was the interest and supplementary financial support of the Royal Commission on the Press. The Royal Commission offered a small grant, sufficient to increase the research sample by some 300 interviews in one city, and also to extend the project's duration by one month. The original conception of the project had assumed that fieldwork would probably be limited to one, or perhaps two, geographical areas, but, in order to meet the requirements of both the Centre and the BBC, the study sampled the population of five English cities. Of course, five cities cannot be regarded as representative of England as a whole, but careful selection allowed the investigation of quite dissimilar complexes of local media in different geographical regions and thus increased the chances of locating and assessing differing audience orientations to local radio.

Although rather daunting, the task of mounting qualitative group discussions in five cities, which approached the country's four corners (and one in the middle)was overcome by having a national fieldwork agency make all necessary preparations. The author then drove round the island, taping and talking, and this arrangement worked so successfully that the same agency, Group Recruitment Ltd., was commissioned to conduct final survey fieldwork in each of the cities.

The qualitative fieldwork, which is described in the following section, continued apace with visits to local radio stations, and also necessary planning, desk research and so forth. In all, ten BBC stations were visited on one or more occasions; Station Managers made the Centre welcome and offered every assistance.[1] Maybe they are a breed with a marked interest in academic research, or perhaps, poor country cousins of the national media and starved of research. Whatever the cause, there was no shortage of indications that wherever the fieldwork was conducted, it would be more than welcome. And interviews with Station Managers were extremely useful in helping the Centre structure the research itself. In order to gain more familiarity with local radio, every opportunity was taken to tune in to stations that can be heard in Leeds (along with Radio Leeds − Blackburn, Humberside, Sheffield, Manchester, and one or two ILR's).

These exercises, plus earlier experience and consultations with other researchers shaped a questionnaire which contained the following major foci:

> Gratifications associated with radio listening as such.
> Gratifications associated with uses of local media.
> Exposure to local radio, regional television, and local press.
> Station images, and aspects of stations that listeners and
>   potential listeners found displeasing.
> Peripheral questions on, for example, favourite programmes/
>   presenters, phone-ins, political bias, and so on.
> Degree of civic involvement, in terms of attitudes, behaviour,
>   social contacts and other demographic particulars (age, sex,
>   social class, occupation, family size, and so on).

Some would argue that such a list is far too wide-ranging: why not a neat two-variable study, local gratifications and civic involvement, for example? Certainly such an approach is tidier and relatively easy (although interestingly, no less costly). Personal experience suggests that, consistent with neither boring nor biasing the informant, fieldwork should generate as much potential information as possible. This means that a larger mass of data can be collected and exploited for information and meaning after the initial central research questions have been answered. Such a data resource is favoured for various reasons, not the least of which refers back to the opening paragraph of this report. Questions answered invariably pose new questions. More often than not the answers to a number of such new questions can be approached with reference to the residual data.

NOTES

[1] The visited stations were: Radio Blackburn (John Musgrave), Radio Bristol (David Waine), Radio Cleveland (Allan Shaw), Radio Humberside (John Cordeaux), Radio Leeds (Ray Beaty), Radio Merseyside (Rex Bawden), Radio Nottingham (Tom Beesley), Radio Oxford (John Pickles), Radio Sheffield (Michael Barton), Radio Stoke (David Harding). Several stations were visited on more than one occasion and opportunities were taken to talk with local radio staff, Broadcasting Councils, and also to observe stations 'in action'.

4 The Qualitative Research

Qualitative work, particularly the conduct of group discussions with target audience groups, has featured in all the Leeds-based uses and gratifications studies. The reasons are forceful and clear enough. The uses and gratifications approach in the first instance emphasises the listener as someone who manipulates broadcast material to his or her own ends; it concerns individual experience and autonomy of action. Little point, then, in the researcher trying to 'think it all out' from a university office; such an approach leads to bias and stereotyping. The place to start is in the home of viewers and listeners who are the experts on their own experience and needs. The researcher's role is to encourage people to talk, and talk, and talk.

Running a group discussion is a fairly personal business. The writer has found that after conducting literally hundreds of groups he is happiest, and his groups are most productive, if they are limited to a maximum of seven individuals. On the other hand, some researchers are at their best with ten, or even twelve informants — it is a matter of personal skills, style and preference. For this reason the following description is just that, a description, not a prescription.

An experienced group recruiter signs up the appropriate number of potential informants, taking care to select people who fit the researcher's stated requirements; apart from specified characteristics such as social class, age, or whatever, it is important that the recruiter should avoid selecting a group of 'good talkers', or people 'especially interested'. Given the correct atmosphere, everybody is a good talker and has his or her own special interest.

Whenever possible, the group discussion itself is held one or two days after recruiting, and in the recruiter's own home. When informants arrive they are greeted by a familiar face, offered tea and biscuits — or sherry, beer, etc. They have been told that the discussion is to be about, in this case, 'Life in Nottingham', or 'Newspapers, Radio, and Television'. The researcher chats for a while, putting people at ease, and then, to ensure that everybody has a chance to speak early on (without this someone will always be a wallflower, sitting tense and miserable, too inhibited to break into the conversation), each person is asked to introduce him— or herself and specify, for instance, which newspapers are taken, or how many children they have. When the last member of the group has spoken the researcher will say something wildly provocative, such as: 'Right, then, who's going to kick off on what it's like to live in Nottingham?' For at least fifteen minutes after that he keeps his mouth shut except to emit the odd grunt of approval. A good group, with a good researcher who uses eye contact, smiles and body position, can run for an hour and cover everything on the researcher's check list without any overt structuring. But usually a few gentle verbal prods and directions are needed to keep everybody on the same topic. Over a sequence of groups some may be wide-ranging and general; others, towards the end of the sequence, are often focused-in on one or two highly specific problems.

The aim is for people to start with obvious superficial comments and gradually to explore more deeply their own experience and beliefs. The informant, after initial inhibitions, usually finds that he or she has a lot to say. The group discussion is almost always a satisfactory experience — 'When can we do it again?' Discussions usually last one to three hours and are tape-recorded in order to allow detailed analysis of language, attitudes and opinions. For this study twenty group discussions were conducted around the country.

In considering the question of local communications gratifications it appeared that the groups might lead toward one, or both, of two possible outcomes, depending upon the researcher's approach. Should the group be encouraged to discuss satisfactions provided by local media, or requirements generated by living in a certain place at a certain time? Allowing that it was always the Centre's intention to do both, it seemed that the latter promised a greater pay-off since it might identify local needs or requirements that were not being satisfied by local media. The first groups then tackled this, and other questions. They were run in Leeds and defined in terms of age, sex, social class and, importantly, duration of residence in Leeds —'old-timers' v. 'newcomers'.

The groups were fascinating and, on many fronts, successful. But they had one disappointing outcome: the idea of having people list (in a general, roundabout, unstructured fashion) requirements by the locality did not pay off. Apart from very obvious superficial needs — bus timetables, shops, sports fixtures, and so on — little emerged from this approach. However, discussion of local media and associated satisfactions was most fruitful. One further point emerged from this first dip, and that was that whilst Radio Leeds, or the Yorkshire Evening Post, had informed one or two members of, say, a new city development, or a fire, other group members had learned of this from other sources, and this helped to put local media in their place. It is obvious really: a great deal of our local information comes from first-hand observation, and, more frequently, fact-to-face (or telephone) communication. Although newcomers might well tune in to their local station, and take the local paper, in order to orient themselves to the locality, even they would also: move around and explore the locality and its amenities; be approached by neighbours or organised groups with useful local information; ask questions of those around them; in some cases visit the library and pick up leaflets, become familiar with local notice boards, and so on. And although the local media provided trips down memory lane for the old-timers, so did a host of other things — friends in the pub, visits to relations, photo albums, and, again, just moving about the city.

It seemed, then, that local media might be a secondary source of local satisfactions, or, as researchers sometimes say in their quaint language, 'a functional alternative' to personal sources of them. The ideal community, with clear social structure and massive face-to-face communication would have little use for local radio, but, by and large, that ideal is long past. If these first group discussions showed that there is more to a locality than its local media, they also emphasised and clarified, for the Centre, the tremendous importance and potential of local media as 'functional alternatives' to a 'community life' which is, in general, fading fast or already gone.

Further groups were run in the five cities which were to be surveyed. Various approaches to group structure were employed; some groups were formed by listeners to local radio, others simply on age, sex and class — allowing listenership to run wild. As it happened, no group contained less than two regular listeners to the local station, and on some occasions (a group in Nottingham of working class women, for example) it proved difficult to dissuade the informants from singing the station's praises, in order to record comment on local press and television broadcasts.

The Centre was well satisfied with this qualitative stage of the research. It promised interesting findings and was by far the most important influence on questionnaire design. For example, groups brought to the forefront certain distinctions and judgements made by several BBC Station Managers: a complex 'image' question to do with such features as friendliness, professionalism, amateurishness, or, again, the rather dramatic effect upon some informants of having a station that broadcast the local accent (no problem, it appeared in Oxford and Bristol, but, oh, how offensive to some of the newly refined ladies of the North and Midlands — and how pleasing to so many others).

The groups, then, shaped the questionnaire in its content and structure. They raised questions to be asked and provided the language that would allow the questions to be meaningful to members of the public. The groups also emphasised (and how!) the enormous differences between our selected cities and their inhabitants. The Centre was encouraged to feel a certain quiet satisfaction in being a Northerner born and bred — although, naturally, some of its best friends are of the South.

5 Sample Questionnaire and Fieldwork Details

Getting a survey into the field (and of all the bits of social science jargon, 'field' deserves a prize for being one of the most inappropriate words, since it usually refers to city streets) involves a complex sequence of decisions. Some are in fact sequential, C being dependent upon B which, in turn, is dependent on A; others form a list that can be tackled in any order; some must be taken or the operation grinds to a halt; others, taken by default, can have unfortunate consequences. And once the agency has been booked and briefings arranged, there is no going back — the researcher is operating in real time. The weeks prior to fieldwork are . . . hectic, and on this occasion they were even more hectic and fraught than usual. The University of Leeds, in its state of perpetual evolution, had taken its own decision: the Centre was to leave home, to move from a charming Victorian rectory and take up residence in the corner of a large building of less charm. It was agreed that the principal researcher would remain unhindered by this move until he had successfully launched his survey. Two days to go, arriving early at the rectory he found his furniture and files waiting — on the pavement. Thus began a bizarre forty-eight hours of phoning, scribbling, and so on, all from the dusty parquet floor of an empty office. Happy days.

The selection of five cities had been made some months earlier. Each of the four people involved in this process (Barton, Blumler, Brown, Emmett) had his own favoured candidates. Indeed the number five itself was a compromise; some wanted more, others less. Whilst it was clear that no sub-set of the existing local radio stations could be said to be representative of local radio as a whole, gross, and necessary simplification of similarities and differences that characterised the stations and their cities allowed some kind of rationale to the final selection.

We could search for geographical balance: North, South, East and West; and counterbalance to the presumed poshness of, say, Oxford, could be found in Liverpool. We could contrast a compact town (Hull) with a more sprawling metropolis (Bristol or Liverpool). The cities could also represent different degrees of 'communications richness' (not to mention financial richness, levels of unemployment, types of employment, and so on), Bristol, a recognised

15

communications centre, but lacking ILR, Liverpool, no home-based television here, but Radio City, a young and apparently thriving new commercially financed local radio station. The final selection pictured England as a lopsided five-spot domino: Hull, Liverpool, Nottingham, Oxford, Bristol. Any selection of five would have had its own quirky consistencies; it was no part of our conscious decision making that produced five university towns, or three major ports!

Although a survey may stand or fall according to its grounding in sensitively conducted qualitative work, group discussions alone are not enough. It is also important that the questionnaire is 'piloted' to make sure that it works, and much more besides. These trial runs allow predictions of the interview's average duration and also a general 'debugging'. For example, a particular statement, taken from a group discussion, may be phrased so that 90 per cent of the sample agree with it. Such a situation is fine for opinion research, but calamitous if the researcher wishes to tap variation in attitudes. Changing the wording of questions — for example, '. . . is the best way . . . ' may become '. . . is a useful way . . . ' — changes the pattern of answers and may make the instrument a more sensitive measure of differences between groups of people. The aim of all this tinkering and 'fine tuning' is to get data which, by statistical jiggery-pokery, can be converted into useful information. 90 per cent agreement means that the researcher can say little about who agrees, what conditions and characteristics are associated with this or that favourable or unfavourable attitude. But, with piloting and tinkering, we can produce an answer which reads: strongly agree — 10 per cent, agree — 40 per cent, neither/nor — 30 per cent, disagree — 20 per cent. Such a distribution is more discriminating; it allows the researcher to investigate other factors which contribute to the informant's feelings. This, it must be emphasised, is not cheating. It is the professional task of producing a suitable set of measuring instruments — when measuring spark plug gaps there is nothing immoral in rejecting a footrule in favour of a feeler gauge.

A draft questionnaire was piloted in Leeds on a hundred members of the public — it transpired that the questionnaire was far too long, and had other problems which were, as they say, 'too numerous to mention'. Major cuts were made; a rambling, repetitive question that took the informant through the previous 'listening day' hour by hour was reduced to four stages: before 9.00 am, 9.00 am to 1.00 pm, 1.00 — 6.00 pm, after 6.00 pm. Some minor questions were dropped, and, of course, in the nature of things, the exercise introduced new questions. This questionnaire was given a further pilot, and final time checks and run-throughs were made. It would work, the Centre decided, crossed its fingers and turned to the problems of printing and collating.

The questionnaire itself is available. It is an interviewer-administered questionnaire and should not be confused with those questionnaires that require 'self-completion'. At no time during the interview is the informant left to read and answer questions; instead an experienced interviewer reads out questions and codes answers. She, the interviewer, is adequately briefed to ensure that she can meet all eventualities. If all else fails, she has the telephone numbers of the Centre, and agency representatives who are always on call. Ideally the interview will run like a reasonably smooth and interesting conversation. Of course, various inventories jar the interview's smoothness, but this is compensated by the satisfaction members of the public find in expressing their opinions to an interested listener. Even though a relatively lengthy interview (it lasted from 15 minutes to 75 minutes and averaged round about 40 to 50 minutes), there was little indication of bored informants. This is consistent with the Centre's usual experience: the public enjoy talking about mass media, and our questionnaires are quite dissimilar in content to run-of-the-mill agency questionnaires. And, of course, high motivation on the informant's part is one of the pay-offs of good preliminary qualitative research and piloting.

At an early stage in the planning the possibility of a split sample, half self-completion, half interviewer-administered had been considered. Such an approach has enormous limitations. For instance, a good self-completion interview could cover only a half of the ground tackled by the present questionnaire. Another problem is that the number of completed questionnaires, or, more accurately, the proportion of completed questionnaires, is reduced. Any drop-out is likely to introduce its own peculiar bias: illiterate and semi-illiterate informants are excluded, those 'pushed for time' are likely to refuse or fail to complete all questions, and so on. It was with relief, then, that the Centre discovered that, with the help of the Royal Commission on the Press, it could complete a survey of 1,300 face-to-face interviews — 200 in each city plus an additional 300 in Liverpool.

All interviewer briefings were conducted by the principal researcher. Hull interviewers were briefed on a Friday night, the remainder on the following Monday and Tuesday. Interviews in each city were completed within fourteen days of briefing. Fieldwork supervisors were appointed who attended briefings, sat in on interviews and substituted for interviewers who, for some reason, were unable to complete their alloted quota of interviews. After the survey, Group Recruitment Ltd. conducted a random 10 per cent back check, using a brief postal questionnaire, to ensure that the survey had been conducted in line with the Centre's wishes. This proved to be the case.

And now, before turning to the survey's results, one final complex of decisions should be considered. 'Who asks what of whom?' Every survey needs a sample, and the question of sampling can be vexed; how vexed depends upon the survey's purpose. Before beginning the survey the Centre had to take three major decisions. Where (in city, city plus portion of region, etc.)? How should sample be defined (matched to city, to nation, to each other)? And, should the proportion of local radio listeners be determined beforehand, be 'built in' as a quota variable?

Our main aims were to assess prevalent satisfactions associated with local media, and to explore some of the possible determinants of these satisfactions. Although reasonably accurate indications of audience size and characteristics would be a welcome spin-off, it was important not to let this consideration influence sample selection to the detriment of our primary concerns. Local radio folklore abounds with stories of record requests from Iceland, Denmark, Edinburgh, and other foreign parts; the actual audience for any one station is spread wide and will always exceed the editorial area. In addition, the sensible technique of sampling from the whole editorial area has its drawbacks, particularly when stations with considerable variation in range of editorial area are being compared with each other.

The Centre's decision was to sample within cities. This would ensure that all respondents were safely within the editorial area, and that the samples would be meaningfully comparable. Of course, it also meant that the respondents would represent a special sub-section of the audience as a whole. This bias is probably most marked in the case of Radio Humberside with its far-flung editorial area and multi-level structure of cities, market towns and villages. In order to make our surveys consistent, we decided to limit interviewing in Humberside to a sample drawn from Kingston-upon-Hull. Again, the description, 'within cities', is not absolutely clear. However, with the help of interviewers, supervisors and maps, a working definition was produced, and wherever possible this was based on the cities' ring-road system. When an estate straddled the ring-road, then interviewers were allowed to work across the whole estate; otherwise they kept on the inside of this sometimes notional boundary. There are many arguments for and against this policy, but perhaps the strongest of them is the proposition that, for most local radio stations, the city is 'where the action is'. And perhaps the results support this assumption since they give a picture of audience satisfaction which is rosier than some research, based on editorial regions, might have suggested.

Having decided to interview within cities, who should be interviewed? Three answers suggest themselves, and each has its own strengths and weaknesses. We could give our interviewers a quota that would produce a sample most suited to statistical exploration. This would involve, say, interviewing as many upper middle class informants as lower working class. Along with the second answer, to base all samples on some notional national sample, it would also mean that each city would be given an identical overall quota. This seemed to be a weakness which would undermine any attempt to estimate the potential audience for a particular local medium and, anyway, fail to make the results from different cities any more comparable than using answer three. The third solution was accepted and involved an attempt to match our quota sample for each city to the population parameters of that city. This at least means that the findings for each city have some immediate face validity. The samples themselves were based on census figures with occasional slight modification to take account of area boundaries. These, where possible, were based on other work such as readership surveys and market research samples.

It could be argued that each of the three suggested solutions is inferior to the use of a random sample in which each member of a defined population (the UK, those who live in a specified town, or whatever) has an equal chance of being included in the research sample. The statistical debate on the values of random versus quota samples is complex. Few social scientists would deny that an adequately mounted, large random sample gives population estimates that are both reliable and valid. However, when the sample is numbered in hundreds rather than thousands quite peculiar results may emerge. For example, a random selection of two hundred city dwellers can give an extremely distorted impression: one hundred and fifty of them might be men. In other words the random sample is random in its generation, but not necessarily representative of the population as a whole. (Given a group of ten Socialists and ten Tories a 5 per cent random sample, that is, one person, is clearly unrepresentative. A 10 per cent sample is hardly any better since the probability of getting two from the same party is only a little less than the probability of picking a Tory and a Socialist. A quota sample would insist on one of each). There are no hard and fast rules governing the decision concerning quota and random samples – unless the sample is extremely large or very small. Many factors intrude such as cost, the availability of information on the population, and so on. In this case an assessment of the strengths and weaknesses of each approach left little doubt that a quota sample was the more appropriate.

A final question also concerns the quota given to each interviewer. So far she would be told to look for a number of people defined in terms of age, social class and sex. But should listenership also be included as a quota variable? The problem is simply stated. If the percentage of listeners was small, our already small sample would locate too few listeners for any worthwhile analysis of their characteristic satisfactions. Ideally, listening would be allowed to 'run wild'. This would reduce bias and also give a clearer indication of the station's actual audience. What to do? The Centre passed the buck; each Station Manager was approached with the problem. In a sense their confidence in the size of their city audience was challenged: if you can only field 10 per cent then the sample will get you about twenty listeners, and there is not much that the Centre can do with that. The Centre was pleased when each of the managers agreed to let listening run wild; interviewers would follow their already complex, interlocking quota, and the Centre held its breath and waited for first indications of the ratio of listeners to non-listeners.

And so it was that Mrs X of Liverpool started the day looking for four males, over 65 years, one from each of four defined social grades. But the question of sampling and quota is not yet exhausted and will recur during the presentation and discussion of results . . .

6 Results

1. CITY CHARACTERISTICS

Although this research does not claim to have done more than it set out to do — study local communications in five English cities — it is hoped that some of the lessons learned might throw light on local communications, particularly local radio stations, as they function in other cities. But that is not to suggest that the results as such are generalisable to other cities. It is clear that each of the five is an individual; indeed, this influenced the Centre's selection. On the other hand, although specific percentages cannot be transferred from one situation to another, relationships between variables, and broader patterns of results, might prove to be the best existing bases for developing working hypotheses about the state of affairs in other localities. Like individual people, cities have their similarities and differences. The perceptive reader who is aware of these similarities and differences will, by the application of sound common sense, appreciate which results have implications that may go beyond the specified cities; he or she will also avoid acting on any temptation to assume that our results, as a whole, are representative of local communications as a whole. The reader is encouraged to maintain a healthy scepticism and, most particularly, to remember that a specific number is based on, say, 200 people answering a specific question: How is the question phrased? If reworded, how would the result be influenced? And, what other factors could have influenced the results?

With these suggestions in mind we turn to 'city characteristics' as portrayed by the surveys. The author assumes that each reader can provide his or her own thumbnail sketches of the five cities and could, if asked to do so, locate the cities on an outline map of the island.

The first set of characteristics was, in fact, built into the study; by providing a 'quota' the Centre predetermined each city's profile in terms of age, sex and social class. Table 6.1 shows these basic demographic representations.

Table 6.1
The Research Sample
(percentage distributions)*

(a)	SEX	Male		Female	
	Oxford	49		51	
	Hull	49		51	
	Liverpool	48		52	
	Bristol	48		52	
	Nottingham	46		54	

(b)	SOCIAL GRADE	AB	C1	C2	DE
	Oxford	16	26	28	30
	Hull	10	20	32	37
	Liverpool	12	16	32	40
	Bristol	10	26	30	35
	Nottingham	13	18	35	34

(c)	AGE	18-25	26-35	36-45	46-55	56-65	65+
	Oxford	14	20	14	14	18	20
	Hull	12	21	18	14	16	19
	Liverpool	12	17	16	18	17	21
	Bristol	14	14	16	20	16	20
	Nottingham	14	16	19	16	16	20

*Unless otherwise indicated, figures in *all tables* are percentages.

Although sex might be said to be more or less the same everywhere, there are differences between towns in terms of both age distributions and 'socio-economic status' — loosely referred to as social grade or social class. The social grade categories are those used in many commercial and academic surveys. Based on income and 'occupational status', they can be crudely interpreted thus: AB — Upper middle, C1 — Middle, C2 — Working, DE — Lower working; ABC1 thus represents the middle classes, C2DE the working classes. The table shows that the proportion of middle class informants ranged from 42 per cent in Oxford to 28 per cent in Liverpool. If, therefore, local radio as a whole appeals to a particular class grouping, then some variation in audience sizes could be due to differences between cities in terms of social structure. Table 6.1(c) shows that the samples were based solely upon adults[1] and ranged from 34 per cent under thirty-five years (Oxford) to 28 per cent under thirty-five years in Bristol.

Given this brief outline of our five samples, it is now appropriate to turn to other ways in which the cities differ. In selecting 'background' variables to cover in the questionnaire, the Centre looked for 'likely candidates', snippets of experience or attitude that might be expected to shape the respondent's orientation to local media. Many such candidates offered themselves, and only a few could be included. Table 6.2 answers one of the most obvious questions: How long had members of the samples lived in their cities? Distinct differences emerge — only 7 per cent newcomers in Liverpool and Nottingham, but 28 per cent in Oxford.

Table 6.2
Years Lived in Locality

	1-10	10-20	20-30	30-50	50+
Oxford	28	16	20	20	16
Hull	17	9	27	25	22
Liverpool	7	11	19	29	35
Bristol	15	18	20	25	22
Nottingham	7	16	22	28	26

And consider the percentage in each city who had lived there thirty or more years: Oxford — 36 per cent, Hull — 47 per cent, Liverpool — 64 per cent, Bristol — 46 per cent, and Nottingham — 54 per cent. These stark numbers are not simply a reflection of age differences between the research samples, and they have implications for a host of other measures. For example, what proportion of each sample had lived in their locality since birth? Oxford — 35 per cent, Hull — 57 per cent, Liverpool — 71 per cent, Bristol — 51 per cent, and Nottingham — 54 per cent. Or, again, what proportions of the samples had been born in or around the city? Oxford — 44 per cent, Hull — 74 per cent, Liverpool — 82 per cent, Bristol — 60 per cent, and Nottingham — 63 per cent; the differences between these figures are a crude indicant of the 'homing' attraction of each city. 19 per cent of the Hull sample left the city, then returned, at the other extreme is Oxford with 9 per cent.

Of course life experience in a city will influence, or be influenced by, the number of friends or relations who live in the vicinity. Tables 6.3 and 6.4 show the distribution of answers to the questions: 'How many of your friends/relations live in or around . . . ? All of them, Most of them, Just a few, or Hardly any? (Qs. 1 and 2)'. The tables have been 'collapsed' to give three levels: 'All or Most, 'Just a Few', and 'Hardly Any or None'.

Table 6.3
Proportion of Friends Living in Locality

	All/ Most	Few	Hardly any/ None
Oxford	65	26	9
Hull	82	14	2
Liverpool	84	10	7
Bristol	77	14	10
Nottingham	82	12	6

Table 6.4
Proportion of Relatives Living in Locality

	All/ Most	Few	Hardly any/ None
Oxford	40	26	34
Hull	72	14	12
Liverpool	71	15	14
Bristol	55	18	25
Nottingham	58	24	17

And, predictably from the earlier figures, there are marked differences, although it is also worth noting the obvious common feature.

The majority of us live in the same area as the majority of our friends and relations. But differences abound, and again the range of these findings highlights them. 40 per cent of the Oxford sample claim to live amongst all or most of their relatives in contrast to 71 per cent of the Liverpool sample. Friendship shows a similar tendency — 65 per cent as against 84 per cent for the same two cities.

A pattern is emerging and perhaps 'In my Liverpool Home' is a song with some justification for its title; on all of these measures Liverpool is at, or near, the 'top' in terms of integration or stability. High percentages of life-long Liverpudlians with most of their friends and relatives in the vicinity suggest the maintenance of a richly inter-connected social network, and, by inference, the distinctive Scouse culture (or cultures) which is given well deserved recognition by the country as a whole. Whilst Oxford, the smallest city in the study (pop: c.112,000), might be regarded as an important storehouse and processing plant for culture, Liverpool (pop: c.600,000) has a centripetality that maintains a strong indigenous culture which is reflected in the city's characteristic accent, verbal fluency and humour.

Other tables showing differences between cities are available and deal, for example, with church attendance, employment, membership of local groups and committees and levels of political involvement. But to round off this first section of results we should turn away from objective, or quasi-objective, measures and consider the sample

87849

25

members' feelings about their cities.

Although it is predictable that the types of measures already presented should be related to respondents' attitudes toward their localities, it is less clear which of these two would be the better predictor of local media use. In order to assess the subjective aspects of involvement in the city, the Centre once more relied, in the first instance, upon group discussions.

The group discussions indicated a simple two part structure to civic attitudes. They also provided a number of statements that could be converted into some kind of a scale of civic involvement or 'feelings about the locality'. Question three was based on a list of facilities and amenities (schools, shops, public transport, access to countryside, and so on). Respondents were asked to specify how important each facility was, using a scale which ran: Very important to me, Important to me, Quite important to me, Not important to me, and, Not relevant to me. The Leeds pilot suggested these to be acceptable labels for the scale. Question four was less concerned with the practical business of living in the city and, instead, looked to a more emotional involvement. Ten statements ('I am proud of this city', 'City people are very genuine', 'It's an interesting place to live with an interesting history', and so on) were read to the respondent who then indicated his or her agreement with each by specifying one of the following four levels: Agree strongly, Agree, No opinion/Uncertain, and Disagree.

Table 6.5(a)
Percentages of City Samples Finding Listed Civic
Amenities Important to Themselves

	Oxford	Hull	Liverpool	Bristol	Nottingham
Public transport	58	67*	73*	59	74*
Libraries/theatres concerts, etc.	63	64	62	68*	62
Cinemas/clubs discotheques	68*	50	48	44	42
Local schools/ colleges	54	54	56	53	50
Road system	83*	74*	76*	77*	63*

Sports facilities/ local sports teams	43	57	55	50	52
Access to country- side/coast	80*	85*	84*	89*	88*
Shopping facilities/ pedestrian precincts	85*	88*	92*	90*	90*
Weather conditions	72*	69*	73*	68*	76*
Local government/ council affairs	62	65	67	65	61

* indicates highest percentages for each city

Table 6.5(b)
Percentage in Each City Agreeing (Agree Strongly and Agree)
with Opinion Statements (Q. 4)

	Oxford	Hull	Liverpool	Bristol	Nottingham
City with real character	89*	77*	77*	87*	77*
It's people are very genuine	46	79*	82*	61	68
New Buildings/roads have improved city	40	75*	50	48	36
Rather live here than elsewhere	59	58	60	68	65
A thriving, busy city	76*	69	60	88*	88*
Proud of this city	73*	75*	63*	74*	70*
Plenty for children/ teenagers to do	22	34	36	58	42

Interesting place to live, interesting history	96*	72	74*	94*	91*
University to be proud of	88*	84*	80*	85*	85*
Very clean city	54	77*	14	62	62

Tables 6.5(a) and (b) provide summary versions of the results showing the percentages in each city agreeing with the opinion statements or finding specified amenities at all important. Table 6.5 (a) reveals a rather consistent pattern across the cities, especially if the first five facilities (those judged important by the largest percentages of the samples and asterisked as such) are inspected. Four amenities are picked out by this criterion in each of the five cities: road system, access to countryside/coast, shopping facilities, and, stretching the definition of 'amenity', weather conditions. But, whilst for the fifth Bristol and Oxford residents hedonistically emphasise leisure time amenities (cinema, theatres, etc.), the three Northern towns, stretching the definition of Northern to include Nottingham, value public transport more often.

More inter-city variation appears in Table 6.5(b). Three statements are most frequently endorsed in all five cities: the city has character, I am proud of this city, and, we have a university to be proud of. Whilst 77 per cent of the Hull sample regard their city (quite realistically) as very clean, Liverpool, ever ready to live up to its choral history ('Dirty Old Town'), produces 86 per cent disagreement with the statement, 'It is a very clean city'.[2] Liverpool and Hull find common cause for satisfaction in having 'genuine people', but, in fairness, some Southerners might find that expression confusing. ('Genuine people' is a common Northern expression possibly best defined as — the type of people who live North of the Trent.)

Clearly these figures provide fuel for many fires, but for the present purpose and for further analysis it is essential to reduce the twenty items into a more manageable array. Instead of twenty numbers per respondent we need to have a smaller number that, in some sense, still contains the meaning and force of the original twenty. Without making heavy weather of it, the procedure is as follows. First, a computer analysis was conducted to see how far responses to the items were related to one another.[3] This showed, as the group discussions had suggested, that these items together formed something akin to a general attitude to the city, the two key, or dominant, items being reliance on public transport and a feeling of pride in the city. A crude but robust scaling was then achieved by allocating numbers to each level of agreement or importance and adding up these numbers for each individual. The computer gave us three scores: total score on Q. 3 (salience of amenities), total score on Q. 4 (opinions about the city), and a score achieved by adding together the two totals. The next stage reduced the now lengthy scales. The distributions were inspected and a decision taken to rescale each of the three measures twice; once into five points and once into three points. This was done so that, on the sample as a whole, roughly equal numbers scored high and low. For the purpose of this report one set of scales will suffice and the simpler three-point scale has been selected. Tables 6.6, 6.7 and 6.8 show the percentage distribution for each city over these three-point scales.

Table 6.6
Importance of Civic Amenities

	High	Medium	Low
Oxford	20	52	28
Hull	22	50	27
Liverpool	30	47	23
Bristol	24	49	27
Nottingham	18	55	28

It will be clear that the items in Q. 3 (Table 6.6) had been scaled in order to give an overall distribution of 25 per cent High, 50 per cent Medium and 25 per cent Low, an exercise that was conducted on a sample of 1,000 respondents (200 from each city), enabling individual city responses to be compared.

In fact, no dramatic differences occur, although Liverpool is apparently a city in which our respondents find amenities important to them slightly more frequently than is the case in the other four cities. However, the utility of this, and the other two scales should not be judged by inter-city comparisons alone, for the scaling was undertaken in order to give more freedom at a later stage in the analysis when scores of civic outlook could be associated with measures of gratifications based on uses of local media.

Table 6.7
Positive Feelings About One's City

	High	Medium	Low
Oxford	26	53	22
Hull	28	54	18
Liverpool	22	52	26
Bristol	34	52	14
Nottingham	27	52	20

Comparison of Tables 6.6 and 6.7 adds to the overall pattern emerging for the cities. Note the position of Liverpool: no great stated pride, a utilitarian, no nonsense parish. Bristol, on the other hand, with a higher ratio of relative newcomers, a place where people go to live — and feel good about it. In fact, only in the case of Liverpool does the percentage of 'High' scorers on the 'practical' amenities scale exceed the percentage of 'High' scorers on the 'pride' scale.

The two measures presented so far have also been combined into an overall measure of involvement which is shown in Table 6.8.

Table 6.8
Involvement in the City

	High	Medium	Low
Oxford	18	58	24
Hull	25	52	23
Liverpool	26	50	24
Bristol	31	50	18
Nottingham	20	54	26

As would be expected from the earlier tables (since Involvement is a combination of the other two scores), we find Bristol and Liverpool leading on this measure of overall involvement. Remember that this and its two fellows feature subjective feelings; because of regional differences (soft, underbelly Southerners, gritty Northerners, and so on) and inequality in the distribution of amenities, the comparisons made are less easily interpreted than those which might be based on 'harder' data such as, say, distribution of income, or unemployment statistics.

The point is that the scales take some of their meaning from the very cities themselves. Pride, for example, may be characteristically expressed by fulsome praise in city A, plain speaking in B, cool understatement in C. Furthermore, our measures of the 'importance' of civic amenities do not discriminate between abundance and dearth or excellence and inferiority, any of which conditions might promote the high salience of a particular amenity.

The utility of these rather more subjective measures in their summarised form is perhaps best judged by their later deployment as predictors of orientation to local media. Nevertheless, the city profiles over the several statements do at least make a start at characterising a public ethos that permeates the outlook of local communication audiences. It seems important to workers in local radio stations and on local newspapers to form some impression of the civic mentality of their own listeners and readers, a topic that, in the absence of survey evidence of the kind presented here, is highly vulnerable to guess-work and the formation of unverified stereotypes. Even so, the data of this section often do tend to confirm certain widely held impressions of differences between English towns. Since Liverpool seems to have made a song, if not a dance, of some of its characteristics, perhaps the last word of this discussion should go to one of its most famous singing sons: 'There is a lot to do in Liddypool, but not all convenience'.

2. EXPOSURE TO LOCAL MEDIA

Measurement in social science is a tricky matter. Take a simple question, 'What time did you go to bed last night?' In a group discussion that question can lead to a debate. Without filling in the 'inbetween' interpretations, 'going to bed' means making supper or a bed-time drink to one respondent and falling asleep to another. Thus A, who went to bed at 10.30, by his own definition, went to bed at midnight by B's definition. Exposure to mass media is similarly complex and, again, in group discussions, where the informant has ample time and opportunity to give explanation and interpretation, one hears: 'Listen? I wouldn't say that I ever really *listen* to radio these days', but that person then explains that he 'hears' the news 'most days'.

It is quite impossible to produce a question that means exactly the same thing to all people. Additionally, different surveys ask differently worded questions of different groups of people (who asks what of whom?). No wonder, then, that measures of exposure to media vary considerably, and that the range of answers in a given survey is so broad. Assuming that the various measures do not have discernible faults, then the most full and accurate picture is likely to emerge from some combination of all available and comparable measures.

This survey featured four measures of exposure to local radio, and each one tends to indicate a rosier picture of BBC local radio audiences than do the routine audience assessments conducted by the BBC Audience Research Department. Exactly why that should be the case will be considered after the results have been presented.

Table 6.9 is based on a direct question: How many days in the average week do you hear anything on local radio?

Table 6.9
Listening to Local Radio (BBC or ILR) in an Average Week

	Never	Less than once a week	Once a week or more
Oxford	32	17	51
Hull	29	3	68
Liverpool	26	14	60
Bristol	50	13	37
Nottingham	18	10	71

Table 6.10 is based on three questions which ask about duration of listening on an average weekday, Saturdays, and Sundays.

Table 6.10
Indication of Audience Sizes for Local Radio Based on Q. 11*

	Oxford	Hull	Liverpool BBC	Liverpool ILR	Bristol	Nottingham BBC	Nottingham ILR
Less than once per week	62	42	64	71	73	43	77
'Listeners'	38	58	36	29	27	57	23

* Table 6.10 shows the arithmetical averages of three sets of exposure figures which relate to weekdays, Saturdays, and Sundays.

Table 6.11 is based on Q. 5, Did you hear radio at all before nine o'clock yesterday morning? and Q. 5c, Which station were you listening to?

Table 6.11
Percentage Claiming to Have Listened to Radio
'Yesterday' Before 9 am

	Oxford	Hull	Liverpool BBC	Liverpool ILR	Bristol	Nottingham BBC	Nottingham ILR
Listen to local radio	16	27	14	7	14	20	6
Listen to any radio	38	57	37	—	50	54	—

Finally, Table 6.12 is based on whether or not the respondent answered Q. 37, which was asked towards the end of the interview and again enquired whether the respondent heard local radio one day a week or more.

Table 6.12
Percentage of Samples Claiming to Hear Local Radio
One Day a Week or More

Oxford	Hull	Liverpool		Bristol	Nottingham	
		BBC	ILR		BBC	ILR
51	67	52	32	37	66	25

Allowing for the different ways in which these figures have been arrived at, they show a reasonable consistency. Note, for instance, that whether or not Independent Local Radio is included increases or decreases the 'listeners' in Liverpool and Nottingham. The most dubious set of figures appears perhaps in Table 6.10, since it, in fact, averages in a rather meaningless way; nevertheless it is acceptable as a further, though frail, indication of relative levels.

Clearly, for those used to BBC 'daily patronage' figures, there is some explaining to do. At first sight the above tables suggest higher levels of listening than anything produced by the BBC Audience Research Department in their routine measurement of local radio audiences. Be of good cheer, a detailed comparison of the two sources points to nothing necessarily untoward. Why does the Audience Research Department of the BBC consistently produce listening figures noticeably lower than those given above? The reader is correct in assuming that the answer is linked to 'who asks what of whom?'

The BBC figures, termed 'daily patronage', refer to a specific day of the week and so can best be compared with Table 6.11. Radio Oxford is taken as an example. During the first quarter of 1976 ARD registered an average daily patronage for Radio Oxford of 10.7 per cent, whereas the equivalent figure from the Centre's study is 16 per cent. Predictions of audience size based upon these two figures, then, would give quite different estimates, though the Centre has not at any time felt any inclination to make such predictions. Possible reasons for this discrepancy fall under two headings and include:

Sample. The BBC uses a national sample with a quota based on national population figures. From that sample respondents living in the Radio Oxford 'editorial area' are included in the calculation of patronage. No attempt is made to produce a sample which corresponds directly to the population living in that area. The BBC sample includes children of five years and over. The BBC operation almost certainly underestimates the number of older listeners who are less likely to be abroad on the streets when interviews are conducted, (as well as the bedridden, of course). The Centre sample, on the other hand, was matched to the city population (smaller than 'editorial area'), excluded anyone under eighteen years and did not limit the chance to be included of any other section of the city population. It should be noted that each of the differences between these two sampling approaches is consistent with the observed differences in listening.

Question. Whilst the BBC Audience Research Department defines patronage on the basis of specific programmes heard, the Centre asked respondents to nominate channels or stations. Understandably, BBC local radio stations have regular opt-out periods when they broadcast the programmes of Radios 1, 2, 3, or 4. Such an opt-out is likely to be introduced thus: 'You are listening to BBC Radio X, your home station, bringing you *Woman's Hour*'. And, of course, once having learned the dial position for Radio X, the listener quite reasonably calls that position on the dial 'Radio X'. Again the implication requires no emphasis: the BBC survey registers someone listening to *Woman's Hour* as a National Listener, while the Centre survey registered a proportion of *Woman's Hour* listeners as Local Listeners. The point has probably been laboured enough; readers will surely agree that different techniques produce different answers, the utility of which must, in the final analysis, be judged by those to whom audience figures are of importance.

After presenting such a detailed analysis of the whys and wherefores of differences between survey results, the writer feels justified in presenting the following tables, on exposure to other media, without any technical or methodological adornment:

Table 6.13
Percentages Claiming to Read Local Evening Papers

	Less Than One Per Week	One-Five Per Week	Every Issue
Oxford	41	18	41
Hull	16	4	80
Liverpool	33	14	53
Bristol	32	24	44
Nottingham	36	14	50

35

Table 6.14
Frequency of Viewing Regional TV News Magazines

	Less than once per week	One to three nights/week	Four + nights per week
Oxford			
BBC	51	22	28
ITV	58	18	24
Hull			
BBC	55	27	18
ITV	33	22	45
Liverpool			
BBC	44	31	25
ITV	34	29	37
Bristol			
BBC	35	26	38
ITV	47	20	32
Nottingham			
BBC	61	20	20
ITV	38	14	47

Finally, we may note that only two of the cities, Oxford and Liverpool, showed any appreciable readership of local weekly newspapers. Asked if they took such a paper 'at least every other week', respondents answered in the following way: Oxford 34 per cent, Liverpool 36 per cent, and, quirkily, each of the remaining cities, 4 per cent. Thus, a probably highly significant form of local media had deep roots in only two of the five cities included in this study. These gross differences in weekly readership do call for further comment, however, and again the explanation given relies in part upon sampling.

Local weeklies, replete with their listings of weddings, whist drives and Brobdingnagian beetroot, photos of football teams and pictures of Pirates of Penzance, are largely a phenomena of the suburbs, dormitory villages and country towns. This stereotype has some semblance to reality and explains, in part, why the inner-city samples of this study included few 'weekly' readers. The exceptions are Oxford, the smallest city, and Liverpool, the largest. Oxford has its

own weekly paper (*Oxford Times*); it is compact enough to have a
local news paper as well as the now common advertising freesheets
that masquerade as newspapers. And Liverpool is large enough to be
carved into separate areas capable of sustaining a weekly, and aided no
doubt by the richness of friendship and kin patterns mentioned in the
preceding section.

Is there a perspective that would enable us to comprehend as a
whole these otherwise separate figures of different media exposures?
A start may be made by noting that, just as we exist in a physical
environment of buildings, houses, shops, roads, trees, parks, etc., and
a social one of contacts with friends, neighbours, relations,
acquaintances and strangers, so too are we located in a
communications environment. This study was focused on certain
major contributors to local communications environments, though an
even more complete analysis would have included community news
sheets, parish magazines, notice boards, face-to-face interaction, etc.

Communications environments may be described in terms of
several dimensions, the most obvious of which are provision and
utilisation. In terms of provision, the notion of communication
'richness' played some part in the selection of our five cities. On such
a dimension, we might contrast Liverpool (TV, two local radio
stations, several local newspapers) with Hull (TV, one local radio
station, one newspaper).

But what of utilisation? Does the provision of numerous local
media mean that the audience for each is spread thinly? Or is it a case
of 'the more the more'? And how does overall utilisation correspond
to other features of the cities concerned? The tables presented in this
section can shed some light on these questions.

Taking each of the presented exposure tables, it is possible to rank
the cities for levels of utilisation, to order them for each medium from
the one with the most numerous listeners/viewers/readers to the one
with the least numerous patrons. In three of the four measures of
exposure to local radio, Hull produces the highest utilisation level,
followed by Nottingham, while on the fourth measure this order of
the top two is reversed. Taking into account the ILR stations in
Liverpool and Nottingham, a rank ordering of local radio audiences
would run as follows: Hull, Nottingham, Liverpool, Oxford and
Bristol. Readership of local evening papers yields the following rank
order: Hull, Bristol, Liverpool, Nottingham, Oxford. BBC TV
(regional news magazines) gives: Bristol, Liverpool, Oxford, Hull,
Nottingham. ITV (regional news magazines) shows: Hull, Liverpool,
Nottingham, Bristol and Oxford. And it will be recalled that
Liverpool and Oxford recorded approximately a third of their samples

as readers of local weekly papers.

We are skating on thin statistics, of course, but it does seem that local media are rather more salient to the people of Hull than, say, to those of Oxford or Nottingham. In fact a little arithmetic play [4] allows the calculation of the following overall ranking of the cities running from the highest total exposure to local media to lowest total exposure: Hull, Liverpool (almost equal), Bristol, Nottingham, Oxford. This order is not in line with that for 'communications richness' on the dimension of provision, nor does it tally with the measured subjective differences between the samples in how their towns were rated for amenity and other characteristics. A glance back at the figures in Table 6.4 for proportions of relatives residing in the locality, however, does suggest the important hypothesis that the preservation of locality-based kinship ties promotes a high rate of local media patronage — and it is also tempting to point out that involvement in local media also seems to correlate rather well with the distance of each city from London!

This section began by arguing the complexity, and related crudity, of exposure measures. And exposure is also crude in another sense, for it tells us nothing whatsoever about the experience of listening, viewing or reading. It is this subjective experience that forms the target of uses and gratifications research. The next section of results takes us a step nearer that target by considering how members of the public react to certain types of local media content.

3. REACTIONS TO THE CONTENT OF LOCAL MEDIA

The next two sections represent a level of analysis midway between headcounting and the charting of audience uses and gratifications.

Table 6.15 is based on answers to question twelve: 'And which programmes or features on BBC Radio . . . do you find most enjoyable and interesting?', a question that was modified and repeated for ILR in Nottingham and Liverpool. Respondents were not shown a prompt card, but group discussion and pilot work allowed the Centre to produce a pre-coded list of likely answers. Each respondent was encouraged to nominate up to three programmes and features. The table presents percentages of listeners, that is nominations of features by those who claimed to listen to local radio one day per week or more. Those items gaining more than 25 per cent nominations are asterisked.

Table 6.15
Programmes or Features Nominated as 'Most Enjoyable and Interesting'

	Oxford	Hull	Liverpool BBC	Liverpool ILR	Bristol	Nottingham BBC	Nottingham ILR[a]
Local news	64*	64*	52*	26*	78*	54*	21
National news	22	13	29*	15	19	14	5
Events/things on	24	20	15	8	29*	14	10
Swop Shop	31*	42*	3	3	26*	31*	—
Quiz/competitions	32*	25*	16	9	11	24	—
Requests/dedications	27*	44*	39*	24	34*	35*	12
Sports	17	14	18	10	19	16	6
Music	18	17	32*	23	20	28*	26*
Interviews	12	17	20	12	27*	24	6

* More than 25 per cent nomination.

[a]The figures for Radio Trent are rather dubious since, at the time of fieldwork, Trent had only just begun to broadcast. Some time will have to pass before stable patterns emerge and the swings and roundabouts of novelty and ignorance settle down.

These data are not presented in order to suggest comparisons between stations in more than a superficial way, but it is worth noting that Bristol, now that we are operating on listeners as such, no longer tails behind the other four stations. Indeed, Bristol receives the highest nomination of all (78 per cent) for its local news service. Table 6.16 is extracted from Table 6.15 in order to highlight preference profiles which are markedly similar from station to station. It shows the five features which received most frequent nomination in each city.

Table 6.16
'Top Five' Features for Each Station

Station						
Oxford	Local news	Quiz	Swop shop	Requests	Events	
Hull	Local news	Requests	Swop shop	Quiz	Events	
Liverpool BBC	Local news	Requests	Music		Nat.news	Interviews
Bristol	Local news	Requests	Events		Interviews	Swop shop
Nottingham BBC	Local news	Requests	Swop shop	Music	Quiz	
					Interviews	

The table shows a very consistent profile, with local news heading the list in every case, and requests coming second in all cases but Radio Oxford, where they came fourth in rank order. Although 'requests' refers to recorded music, which need have no 'local flavour', the request, or dedication, feature of local radio has an important part to play in the production of a local 'feel' to radio. It is requests that ensure that an endless stream of local names and addresses is broadcast. It will be reported below that a quite sizeable proportion of our samples had in fact heard their names mentioned on local radio. 'Music', on the other hand, need not reflect this local element, but clearly quizzes, 'events' and 'swop shop' do.

This rough classification into local and non-local features reveals, beneath the overall consistency, an atypical patterning in the top five of Liverpool, for here National News and 'music' have displaced the more localised emphasis on swop shops, events and quizzes. But it is the consistencies of Table 6.16 that should be most stressed. The following two items appear in every list: Local news and requests; four out of five occurrences for: 'Swop shop'; three out of five for quizzes, interviews and the 'What's on' events type of item. Radio City, the Liverpool commercial radio station, has for its top five: Local news, requests, music, National News, and interviews, a profile which, oddly enough, is shared by the Liverpool BBC stations (although Radio Merseyside gains higher percentage nominations as shown in Table 6.14).

Question 22 allows a similar sort of table to be compiled for local evening newspapers: 'Which parts of (LOCAL EVENING) do you make a point of reading?' Again no prompt card was given, with the interviewer encouraging one or two answers to this question. Table 6.17 shows the results.

Table 6.17
Parts of Local Evening Paper 'Readers' Make a Point of Reading

	Oxford	Hull	Liverpool	Bristol	Nottingham
Sports	34*	32*	40*	45*	33*
Front page/ news headlines	75*	74*	80*	76*	74*
Advertisements	46*	32*	36*	47*	23
Letters	27*	13	24	28*	26*
Births, deaths & marriages	29*	44*	18	28*	26*
TV/radio/cinema	28*	38*	43*	50*	40*
Women's page	13	8	16	18	3
Horoscope	6	7	21	21	12
Other	14	20	18	13	13

* More than 25 per cent nomination.

Again, as with radio, news predominates; and again some similarity between the cities is apparent. The importance of news, sports and leisure guides in all cities is quite striking and says much about the functions of local dailies. Consider, however, the odd inconsistencies. Why should Liverpool drop down on that classic column for Births, Deaths and Marriages? One possible answer is found in the reported city characteristics. Liverpool is a city thick with kith and kin, facilitating a dense network of face-to-face interactions. Perhaps, then, there is no need for the Liverpudlian to survey that column in order to locate signals of joy and distress amongst those he or she once knew, for the column might usually be last with the news. (It would be interesting to compare these figures with , should they exist, similar ones for Liverpudlians who have been rehoused and now suffer from ruptured networks of interaction.) But why should Nottingham and Hull produce markedly low nominations of the 'Women's Page'? Perhaps this is a reflection of the newspapers of those cities as such rather than readership.

Advertisements, the economic life blood of newspapers, perform well in this table, only receiving less than 25 per cent nomination in Nottingham. Overall, however, as with local radio, it is a pattern of inter-city consistency that emerges most clearly from this table. On the other hand, a curious and pleasingly erratic sequence of numbers follows the legend, 'Horoscope'. The two large west-coast cities both produce 21 per cent claims for 'Horoscope' contrasted with 7 per cent and 6 per cent in the smallest cities of Hull and Oxford. Could this be due to Celtic blood, the Gulf Stream, or even the excellence of those who write astrological predictions? Anyone who would like to see further work on this fascinating problem is advised to contact the writer . . . with offers of financial assistance. [5]

Since Local news features so strongly in both these results and in interviews with local broadcasters, it is worth seeing if respondents felt that they had learned anything about local affairs, specifically local politics. Table 6.18 is based on Q. 15: 'Would you say that BBC Radio . . . has made you more aware of local politics and council affairs?' Such a question has more to do with the felt satisfactions of listening than with measured effects; it should not be assumed that the figures necessarily represent learning gains.

Table 6.18
'Would You Say BBC Radio X Has Made You More Aware
of Local Politics and Council Affairs?'

	Yes	No	Don't know
Oxford	68	28	4
Hull	47	46	7
Liverpool	39	53	8
Bristol	54	45	1
Nottingham	42	45	13

The figures are, of course, percentages of listeners rather than of the samples as a whole. The differences will doubtless be of interest to some readers, but should be handled with care, since, for example, an already well-informed populace will not be made 'more aware' by the introduction of a new medium. Perhaps, then, the apparent extremes of Oxford and Liverpool reflect not some measure of the stations' emphasis on civic affairs but the relative involvement of the two sets of citizens in local politics. However, without additional information this question cannot be resolved, and it does seem likely that such distinct differences are, at least in part, a result of broadcast treatment of civic politics.

Bias is in the eye of the beholder and that is both a blessing and a bane for the researcher. In this report it is seen as a blessing, although the results of two questions included in this survey about bias in local broadcasting cannot rightly be considered inflammatory or even very exciting.

Table 6.19
Does Radio X Favour the Views of:

	People	Council	Business	All/none	Don't know
Bristol	37	4	2	6	51
Oxford	47	6	4	5	38
Nottingham	24	5	2	16	53
Hull	55	7	3	4	31
Liverpool	28	2	1	11	58

Table 6.19 suggests that most listeners are either reserving their opinion on this question or genuinely don't know. Presumably broadcasters will be well-satisfied with the tag 'people's medium' which is quite appropriate on the basis of these data, and especially so in the instances of Radio Humberside and Radio Oxford. When asked about party political bias the stations were given a clean bill of health, 'no bias' being reported by the following percentages of listeners: Oxford 90 per cent, Hull 84 per cent, Liverpool 95 per cent, Bristol 96 per cent, and Nottingham 94 per cent.[6]

BBC local radio stations rely on a small number of programme presenters and announcers, and radio, an 'intimate' medium, must needs have performers who can generate a sense of rapport over the air. The survey looked at two aspects of this question: presenters' ages and presenters' origins. In terms of age the great majority of all listeners thought that their local presenters were neither too young nor too old. (Percentage of listeners thinking that the age of their local radio announcers was 'about right': Oxford 90 per cent, Hull 90 per cent, Liverpool 84 per cent, Bristol 99 per cent, and Nottingham 95 per cent.) But 'genuine locals', an emotive term, produces a rather more subdued enthusiasm except in the case of Liverpool. 'Scouse' is, of course, a distinctive city accent whereas the other cities echo to the sound of modified regional accents which may make the recognition of broadcast 'genuine locals' a more difficult task.

Table 6.20
'In General, Do You Think the People on BBC Radio X
are Genuine Locals?'

	Yes	No	Don't know
Oxford	51	31	18
Hull	58	28	14
Liverpool	74	7	19
Bristol	57	16	27
Nottingham	45	24	31

It has been suggested that people often read local weeklies for the pleasure of seeing their own name in print (if the name is correctly spelt and decipherable; according to one member of a Liverpool group discussion a typical greeting to the dirty-handed Scouse is, 'See you've been reading the paper then'). What percentage of city dwellers in this study had been mentioned by name on radio or in the local paper? The answer is shown in Table 6.21.

Table 6.21
Percentage of Listeners/Readers Mentioned by Name
in Local Media

	BBC Local Radio	Local Evening Paper
Oxford	30	37
Hull	16	32
Liverpool	12	31
Bristol	18	40
Nottingham	16	40

The local evening is an old timer, and for many their first mention is in Births-Deaths-Marriages. The high level for local radio is an indication of the involvement of listeners in their local station, often reflected in record requests and 'phone-ins' but it is also a function of audience size. The extremes of Oxford and Liverpool coincide with the extremes of city populations already mentioned.

By emphasising the viewpoint of regular listeners and readers this section has possibly been pleasing to the broadcaster. The next section discusses the image of local radio and draws on the views of the whole samples, listeners and non-listeners alike.

4. IMAGES OF LOCAL RADIO

So far local radio has performed rather well in the survey and although the data reported are based on questions that are positive in wording, a far more dismal picture could have emerged. In this section we consider some of the negative sides of the local broadcasting coin and present data generated by the samples as a whole rather than relying solely on those who, by virtue of being regular users, share a degree of commitment to local media. There is a qualitative difference between a regular listener's stated reasons for enjoying a programme, and the reasons a non-listener gives for not listening. A decision not to do something, or to dislike something which is beyond our experience, is difficult to change. ('Eat your cabbage.' 'I don't like cabbage.' 'You've never tasted it.' 'That is because I don't like it.')

An animal dominated by patterns of habit, imposed work patterns, unconscious motivations, and so on, need not actually take decisions to avoid something — it can just happen that way. On the other hand, we are often able to justify our non-decision: 'I've never really thought much about it, but I suppose I've never done it because it's so messy . . . and it can't be good for your health can it?' This is an example of 'it' having an image based on minimal experience, or no experience at all. Although — and let us leave 'it' now and turn to local radio — non-listeners will typically have an image of their local station, listeners will tend to have a more highly formed one. For this reason the following tables could cause some confusion if the wrong 'model' is applied. It should be remembered that whilst a non-listener may have three reasons for not listening, a regular listener may have four reasons for not listening more often; furthermore a regular listener could be irritated by local radio more often than a non-listener.

Table 6.22 presents data on irritations and reasons for not listening and is based on Q. 17, [asked of everybody, listeners and non-listeners]:

> Here are some things that people have told us when asked why they didn't care to listen to local radio very much (informant is given a prompt card bearing eleven statements). Please look them through. Now just give me the numbers of any comments that help to explain why you might sometimes be put off listening to local radio.

The table shows distributions of answers for all stations in the five cities, and the top five 'negatives' are asterisked for each station. Since the respondent could give as many, or as few, reasons as he or she liked, each number on the table could range from zero to one hundred per cent.

Table 6.22
Reasons for Not Enjoying Local Radio

	Oxford	Hull	Liverpool BBC	Liverpool ILR	Bristol	Nottingham BBC	Nottingham ILR
Ignorant of schedule	33*	34*	27*	24*	38*	35*	26*
Too much pop music	20*	20*	37*	38*	18*	30*	30*
Trivial	30*	33*	24*	20*	16*	36*	26*
Amateurish	14*	25*	12*	11*	10*	17*	17*
Lacks big name stars	11*	10	6	6	8*	10	5
Local accent 'overdone'	3	20*	17*	15*	7	2	1
Local affairs uninteresting	8	10	4	3	4	17*	11*
Too much politics	8	6	6	4	3	12	8
Highbrow	2	10	8	6	6	4	2
Not local enough	4	6	3	2	3	—	—
Programmes don't stay on one topic	4	12	7	7	3	5	2

The first thing to note about this table is that no single statement ever receives more than 40 per cent nomination. The second thing to notice is the consistency from station to station. All seven stations include the same four statements in their 'top fives': 'Too much pop music', 'Too much gossip and trivial talk', 'Too amateurish', and, 'Ignorant of schedule' (presented on the prompt card as 'There are probably some programmes I would enjoy, but I don't know when they are on'). A further three stations (in Liverpool and Hull) are criticised for 'overdoing the local accent', and 17 per cent of the Nottingham sample link Radio Nottingham with the comment, 'Local affairs don't interest me all that much'.

One man's Led Zeppelin is another man's Victor Sylvester — so what does 'too much pop' mean? The unavoidable answer is that it means whatever the individual respondent takes it to mean, but, regardless of 'pop's' interpretation, a sizeable proportion of our sample link local radio with pop — and don't like it. The cliche would have it that you cannot please all of the people all of the time, and, as usual, the cliche is correct. The reasons given for not listening more often (they were taken from group discussions) do not, in general, suggest immediate action. Changing the type of music would activate a 'too much pop' circuit in some other section of the population, and cutting back on local accents would probably increase the incidence of 'not really local enough'. But one item has definite implications, and that is the one in Table 6.22's top row — 'ignorant of schedule'.

Elsewhere[7] the writer has discussed various characteristics of media which influence the audience members 'functional orientation'. Of particular importance is the range of material the medium makes available, and also the degree of control over selection of material that is offered the audience. For example, a longplaying record broadcast on radio has the same range of content as the identical record played at home on a deck, but at home the listener can reorganise that content because he or she has control over its selection. Again, a newspaper and a radio news programme may cover the same issues, but the reader is able to move from one to the other in his own desired sequence.

Print and recorded music give more control to the user than do television and radio; this is unavoidable, but the more a listener is aware of broadcast schedules the more quasi-control he or she has over selection. Increasing this awareness, and thus increasing quasi-control, could modify the audience member's 'functional orientation' to radio — in other words, it would allow him or her to make a more adequate use of the medium in terms of uses and gratifications. And beneath the question of schedule ignorance is another core factor of local radio philosophy — mixed programming, in all its guises. This research was not directed to the question of whether or not stations should fill their air time with specific highly defined programmes, or with magazines which move from one topic to another, for that is more a question for the creator of broadcast material than for the researcher. But the broadcaster's position on that question should relate to the ease, or difficulty, of publicising specific content sequences.

Responses to the 'gossip, trivial, amateurish' items are also of interest. In this context they are obviously seen as negative attributes; on the other hand, many listeners regard the 'amateur' character of some local radio as being synonymous with the station's 'friendliness'. This issue was raised in almost every group discussion and it contributes to Table 6.23, which presents 'image' data for each station. The results are taken from Q. 18 which was asked of all respondents:

> For this question I shall read out fifteen words. After each one I would like you to tell me whether you think it applies to any of the local and national radio stations. Even if you don't often listen to the station you might have some impression of it. Here is the first: CHEERFUL. Which, if any, of the stations do you think are cheerful?

In asking this question no attempt was made to prompt the respondents nor to remind them of stations. The checklist was based on words frequently used in group discussions when talking about radio in general and local radio in particular.

Table 6.23
Percentages of Whole Samples Relating Check List
'Image' Items to LR Stations

	Oxford	Hull	Liverpool		Bristol	Nottingham	
			BBC	ILR		BBC	ILR
Local	84*	90*	73*	63*	82*	83*	47*
Regional	72*	76*	54*	40*	70*	59*	33*
Friendly	42*	62*	49*	30*	31*	56*	20*
Interesting	42*	54*	32*	19	26*	55*	16
Amateur	39*	61*	24	27*	26*	28	32*
Cheerful	36*	46	41*	28*	24*	52*	20*
Amusing	36*	48*	38*	23	18	54*	16
Working class	23	68*	36*	31*	26*	43*	28*

Professional	20	11	19	10	18	19	7
Trivial	17	23	23	28*	8	22	25*
Middle class	14	11	7	4	14	14	2
Boring	12	13	13	13	7	12	2
Serious	11	6	5	2	10	6	3

Whilst some members of the public complain that local radio is not nearly local enough, all stations are recognised as local and, to a lesser extent, regional. For this reason, the top seven items are asterisked on this table. In passing, it is worth noting that the ILR stations score less highly on the 'local' dimension, a consequence, no doubt, of emphasis on music and national newscasts, amongst other factors.

Ignoring the items, 'local' and 'regional', what do the stations have in common? The top five for each station includes 'friendly', and, if the analysis is limited to BBC stations, 'interesting'. Table 6.24 spells out the dominant image of each BBC station.

Table 6.24
Top Five Image Items for Each Station

Oxford	cheerful	friendly	amusing	amateur	interesting
Hull	friendly	working class	amusing	amateur	interesting
Liverpool	cheerful	friendly	working class	amusing	interesting
Bristol	cheerful	friendly	working class	amateur	interesting
Nottingham	cheerful	friendly	working class	amusing	interesting

Again consistency is the keyword, and it is difficult to avoid reintroducing the 'people's medium' tag. Of course, this is a general image, a best approximation for cross-sections of the five groups of citizens. Embedded in Table 6.23 are all those who evaluate their local stations as 'boring' and 'trivial'. And implicit to Table 6.23 is the assumption that if 50 per cent think that Radio X is cheerful, a further 50 per cent were not moved to describe it in that way (nor would they necessarily think the station 'miserable').

If the overall impression generated by these tables is one of consistency, however, it must also be recognised that they contain a fair number of inter-city differences. Consider, for example, the class aspect of these images: 68 per cent of the Hull sample describe their station as working class, whereas the corresponding figures for Oxford and Bristol are 23 and 26 per cent, respectively. Nottingham and Hull are both seen as 'amusing' far more frequently than is Bristol, and Liverpool is rather low on being 'interesting' when compared with other BBC stations. It is also worth noting that the ILR stations have less pronounced images and possibly less favourable ones.

This and the preceding section of results has moved away from bare listening figures and begun to explore in more detail the experience of exposure, reasons for not listening, and, latterly, the 'personality' of local radio stations. All of this has been by way of background or introduction to the research project's main target of investigating gratifications associated with local media use. The next section moves onto target and deals with local radio in the context of radio listening as such.

5. GRATIFICATIONS ASSOCIATED WITH LISTENING TO RADIO.

That news media offer the user an opportunity to, as it were, keep an eye on what is going on around the world is rather obvious. And one of the satisfactions, or gratifications, measurably associated with watching television news has been labelled 'surveillance'. Being somewhat egocentric creatures, we want to know, first, that nothing untoward has occurred in our immediate environment (that in a psychological sense rather than a geographical one — if we plan a trip to Workington, then Workington becomes part of our psychological environment, we would like to know how things are over there). An early morning need for local information is clearly advantageous to local radio audience building. But, for the moment, it acts as a point of entry to two highly specific questions embedded in the present investigation: How time-specific are certain gratifications? And, are they patterned through the day? The questions are of some interest to the Centre and serve as a starting point for presenting the radio audience gratification results.

The questions were tackled using six fairly typical gratification statements: 'It took my mind off other things', 'It was like a friend calling in', 'It helped to keep me cheerful', 'It kept my mind active', 'I got involved in it', and 'It helped to keep me going'. These statements were derived from group discussions and earlier work. Although typical, they were not selected in order to represent listening gratifications as a whole.

Questions five to eight on the questionnaire took the respondent through the previous day's listening, the day being broken into four segments: before 9 am, 9 am to 1 pm, 1 pm to 6 pm, and 6 pm to midnight. Anyone who had listened, even if only for a couple of minutes, during one or more of those periods was asked, for the appropriate period, part (f) of the question: 'On this card are some things people have said about listening to radio. Do any of these statements relate to how you felt about radio yesterday (morning, forenoon, etc.)?'.

For the Centre this was in part an exploratory approach to see how people cope with gratification statements linked to actual periods of exposure, rather than to the medium as a whole, or specific programmes — those being the most frequently employed methods. And would these fairly vague statements indicate any kind of patterning through the day? The answer, it appears, is a vague 'Yes'.

Taking enormous liberties, and thumbing his nose at finnickety statisticians, the writer presents a table based on all respondents (excluding 300 Liverpudlians). (For many uses adding together the five city samples would lead to spurious conclusions, but in this case it is, at least, illustrative.) Table 6.25 shows the overall percentages of listeners who endorsed the six gratification statements at different times of day.

Table 6.25
Daytime Variation in Six Selected Gratifications
Associated with Radio Listening

	Before 9 am	9 am − 1 pm	1 pm − 6 pm	6 pm − MN
Took my mind off other things	17	19	17	19
Like a friend calling in	8	11	9	11
Helped to keep me cheerful	35	38	37	30
Kept my mind active	27	21	24	25
Got involved in it	7	11	10	16
Helped to keep me going	17	21	20	13

The results suggest a general 'helping to cope' function of radio, but that is a consequence of using selected items. Our time patterning hypothesis gains some little support from this exercise. For example, the two statements, 'helped to keep me cheerful' and 'helped to keep me going' (related conditions as any ITMA fan will recall) follow a similar course through the day. They increase as the morning passes and decline with the sun. 'Involvement', on the other hand, shows a gradual increase as time passes, and 'kept my mind active' is bow-shaped with a high point in the early morning. Of course, other items might have been selected that would, by their nature, emphasise day time variation — 'wakes me up', 'I find it relaxes me', 'lets me know how the day is progressing', but they would not have provided such a stringent test of the time-base hypothesis. These results are encouraging enough to suggest that future studies could usefully address the question in greater detail. For now, it is enough to note that not only does an audience's constituent parts change throughout the day, but that some of the requirements that audience members bring to listening also vary as the day progresses. An obvious point perhaps — but research often involves complex, expensive, procedures in order to 'objectify' what most people already know. [8]

The study now enters one of the areas that shaped its conception: local radio was located in two contexts — that of national radio and that of local media of communication. In the first context emphasis is obviously placed on the gratifications associated with radio listening as such, there would be little point in demonstrating that the good people of Hull receive more news of local affairs from Radio Humberside than they do from Radio 4. The second context emphasises local satisfactions since, again, each medium has obvious advantages and disadvantages (try lighting the fire with Radio Humberside, or, for that matter, reading *The Hull Daily Mail* whilst driving to work).

In this first major analysis of gratifications, we place local radio alongside national radio and ask how they compare as sources of 'listener gratification'. Perhaps such a comparison seems unfair; like comparing Concorde with a Tiger Moth it may seem beyond dispute which is the faster. And it is certainly beyond dispute that national radio has a more adequate budget and facilities than local radio, that national radio is staffed by more experienced personnel, that it is more likely to feature contributions from the 'big names' of show business, international affairs and the arts. But many of us, (perhaps an increasing proportion of the population) could nevertheless yearn for that Tiger Moth.

The six gratification statements listed in Table 6.25 are in no sense biased towards local or national radio. and although individual stations may be more likely to provide one satisfaction than another, the statements are directed to radio as a whole and to listening as such. The same applies to the fourteen statements that were used to assess local radio in a 'listening' context. No attempt was made to 'highlight' local radio at this stage: the statements were taken from earlier research and those parts of discussions that focused on the satisfactions derived from listening as such. The inventory of statements was administered to respondents who listened to radio, any station, one day per week or more frequently.

Q. 10: Here are some more statements about radio and the kinds of satisfactions you can get from listening. I'll read them out one

54

by one. After I read the first one tell me whether you agree with
it.

After each statement the interviewer recorded 'agree' or 'disagree'. If
'agree', she asked the respondent which station or stations was most
relevant to the statement in the listener's opinion. No check list of
stations was offered, and at this stage in the questionnaire no detailed
questions had been asked about local radio and therefore the
respondent was not 'primed' to nominate one channel any more than
another. The results are given in the lengthy Table 6.26 below, the
first part of which is extracted here for explanatory purposes.

Extract from Table 6.26

City	R1	R2	R3	R4	BBCLR	ILR
Gratification						
(a) I find that the Liverpool	16	30	2	8	39	24
radio is good						
company Nottingham	22	30	2	9	46	19
Oxford	18	28	10	18	34	—
Hull	36	22	4	14	42	—
Bristol	36	40	8	19	24	—

Before attempting any interpretation of the table the reader should
be clear about the following points:

The figures are percentages of full samples (200, not just
listeners).
The figures are not measures of listening, but they are influenced
by the proportion and distribution of listeners in each sample.
Respondents could nominate any, or all, stations, therefore the
answer, 'R1, R2' contributes equally to both columns and rows
summate to 100 per cent plus.

Taking the first line of the example, 16 per cent of the Liverpool
sample nominated R1 as being 'good company', while 30 per cent
nominated R2. A proportion of these two groups is common and
formed by those respondents who nominated both R1 and R2. 2 per

cent nominated R3, 8 per cent R4, 39 per cent BBC local radio and 24 per cent ILR. In fact, this first item reveals a pattern of gratification that is quite consistent. BBC local radio tends to dominate in all cities except Bristol, where R1 and R2 gain the highest percentage nominations. In the two cities with commercial radio, R1 and R2 show a rather below-average frequency of endorsement, R3 gains minimal recognition, and R4 also rarely approaches the levels of Rs 1, 2 or local radio. This example also shows some inter-city patterning that will become familiar, particularly the peaking of R3 in certain reputed centres of 'high' culture, Oxford and Bristol. With these suggested consistencies in mind the reader can now approach the rather lengthy Table 6.26 before consulting the summaries and further comment that follow.

Table 6.26
Listening Gratification Profiles for National and Local Stations

Q. 10: Here are some more statements about radio and the kinds of satisfactions you can get from listening. (Informants were asked to link each statement to any, all, or none of the named stations.) Entries are percentages of total samples (200).

Stations

	City	R1	R2	R3	R4	BBCLR	ILR
(a) I find that the radio is good company	Liverpool*	16	30	2	8	39	24
	Nottingham*	22	30	2	9	45	19
	Oxford*	18	28	10	18	34	—
	Hull	36	22	4	14	42	—
	Bristol*	36	40	8	19	24	—
(b) It helps to keep me cheerful	Liverpool*	14	24	1	5	38	26
	Nottingham*	22	29	2	8	43	16
	Oxford	14	26	7	10	28	—
	Hull*	34	18	2	9	50	—

		Stations					
	City	R1	R2	R3	R4	BBCLR	ILR
(b)	Bristol	34	38	4	15	20	—
(c) I rely on the time	Liverpool	12	18	—	4	28	15
	Nottingham	20	22	1	5	25	8
	Oxford	12	20	6	10	22	—
	Hull	27	18	—	9	41	—
	Bristol	23	29	2	10	16	—
(d) When I listen to radio I can forget my problems	Liverpool	7	12	1	4	19	9
	Nottingham	6	12	—	3	22	6
	Oxford	5	13	2	4	14	—
	Hull	10	10	1	7	23	—
	Bristol	18	20	3	12	12	—
(e) It keeps me in touch with what is going on	Liverpool*	14	19	—	14	38	22
	Nottingham*	10	22	—	9	50	18
	Oxford*	10	25	6	24	36	—
	Hull*	18	16	—	12	55	—
	Bristol*	22	32	4	18	25	—
(f) Listening to radio takes my mind off other things	Liverpool	10	18	2	6	22	13
	Nottingham	8	14	—	4	26	8
	Oxford	11	18	4	11	24	—
	Hull	21	30	4	14	18	—

	City	R1	R2	R3	R4	BBCLR	ILR
(f)	Bristol	21	30	4	14	18	—
(g) Some of the regulars on radio have become like friends to me	Liverpool	8	12	1	4	22	12
	Nottingham	3	8	—	2	21	2
	Oxford	10	16	2	8	17	—
	Hull	9	8	—	6	28	—
	Bristol	15	18	1	8	12	—
(h) I find it relaxing to listen to radio	Liverpool*	17	26	—	8	34	20
	Nottingham	14	25	2	4	37	16
	Oxford*	11	26	7	15	29	—
	Hull	30	23	3	12	44	—
	Bristol	30	38	5	17	20	—
(i) It keeps my mind active	Liverpool	12	18	1	6	28	14
	Nottingham	12	23	2	8	35	22
	Oxford	10	20	10	20	24	—
	Hull*	18	13	1	13	46	—
	Bristol*	22	29	4	20	23	—
(j) It helps to pass the time	Liverpool	17	20	2	7	33	17
	Nottingham	14	22	1	6	40	16
	Oxford*	14	23	4	10	29	—
	Hull	22	19	1	8	19	—

	City	R1	R2	R3	R4	BBCLR	ILR
(j)	Bristol	30	32	4	12	19	—
(k) It keeps me up date with current affairs	Liverpool	13	22	2	12	33	20
	Nottingham*10		22	1	10	45	12
	Oxford*	10	22	3	24	36	—
	Hull*	16	15	1	14	56	—
	Bristol*	17	28	3	21	23	—
(l) I get really involved with some of the programmes	Liverpool	6	10	—	4	20	11
	Nottingham	4	9	—	4	20	1
	Oxford	6	14	4	10	18	—
	Hull	8	6	4	8	31	—
	Bristol	10	18	3	16	14	—
(m) It helps to keep me going	Liverpool	12	16	—	4	25	16
	Nottingham	12	20	—	2	37	12
	Oxford	11	16	4	10	24	—
	Hull	18	10	1	5	28	—
	Bristol	25	32	2	10	14	—
(n) It lets me know what other people think about issues of the day	Liverpool*	11	20	1	10	35	20
	Nottingham* 9		29	—	8	42	10
	Oxford*	7	22	7	25	35	—
	Hull*	16	13	2	13	54	—

	Stations						
	City	R1	R2	R3	R4	BBCLR	ILR
(n)	Bristol*	17	28	2	20	26	—

It would seem, then, that the 'Tiger Moths' do rather well for themselves. Why should local radio be so predominant? First, it should be re-emphasised that at this point in the interview respondents had no sound reason to assume that the survey would feature local radio any more than national radio. There is no reason to assume that respondents were biasing their answers in order to please the interviewer. Nor does it seem at all probable that the results were shaped by random fluctuations in response; the pattern is far too consistent for such an interpretation. There is, then, something to be explained. And there are a number of legitimate explanations which, taken together, account for local radio's admirable performance in this context of 'listening gratifications'.

First, and by now predictably, it should be recalled that these percentages are based upon defined groups of people and the percentages have no meaning whatsoever unless they are related to the people who generated them. Our samples, being city dwellers, are obviously more likely to find satisfaction in local radio than any general national sample. Furthermore our samples omit the younger city dweller; had we included adolescents and children, then the picture might have been quite different and would probably have been characterised by a move away from local radio towards R1 and ILR.

Second, we should be aware that whilst a research study can be based upon the splitting of local radio into two contexts, for the listener these contexts will normally be interfused. Our adaptations to life are characterised by an attempt to maximise satisfaction; we seek an interesting job which is also well paid and allows contact with people who are 'easy to get along with'. The ideal wife, it has been said, combines the functions of mistress, housekeeper and friend. The listener who 'uses' local radio for specific 'local satisfactions' will also seek, while doing so, certain more general satisfactions that might equally well have been provided by national radio.

Third, it is at least arguable that the local flavour of local radio could facilitate more generalised 'listener gratification' for some members of the public. The frequent use of local expressions, local accent, and references to local institutions, affairs and places allows such listeners a degree of contact with local radio that is missing when he or she tunes in to national broadcasts, even though what is mainly

60

wanted may be some form of non-parochial satisfaction.

Finally, local radio is unique in its commitment to 'mixed programming'. In a typical day the local station gives you a bit of most things rather than a lot of music (high or low-brow) or a lot of talk. For some people, local radio can create a quite justifiable 'button apathy'. If the local station can provide just one service not provided on a national channel (local news), then there is perhaps little reason to fiddle with the set throughout the day. Mixed programming will ensure that the listener hears a variety of programmes, including national news, time checks and so on.

Some of these arguments are further returned to below, but at this stage it is worth asking which 'listening gratifications' local radio stations best serve? Table 6.27 shows the top fives for each local station, a 'plus' indicating that the particular item is included amongst the specified city's top five gratifications.

Table 6.27
Top Five Listening Gratifications Associated with Each Station

CITY

Gratification statement	Oxford	Hull	Liverpool	Bristol	Nottingham
(e) It keeps me in touch with what is going on.	+	+	+	+	+
(n) It lets me know what other people think of the day.	+	+	+	+	+
(a) I find the radio good company.	+		+	+	+
(k) It keeps me up to date with current affairs.	+	+		+	+
(b) It helps to keep me cheerful.		+	+		+
(h) I find it relaxing to listen to radio.	+		+		

61

CITY

Gratification statement	Oxford	Hull	Liverpool	Bristol	Nottingham
(i) It keeps my mind active.			+		+
(j) It helps to pass the time.		+			

The table shows that for all five local radio stations, item (e) 'It keeps me in touch with what is going on' appears amongst the top five gratifications. On the other hand item (h), 'I find it relaxing to listen to radio', is in the top five of only two stations: Oxford and Liverpool. And (j), 'It helps to pass the time', only features in the top five of Radio Oxford. Fourteen items were included in this instrument, and yet all five stations' top five gratifications are contained in the subset of eight shown in the table. Again, then, there is a degree of consistency across the cities.[9] In fact all five cities feature (e), 'It keeps me in touch with what is going on', and (n), 'It lets me know what other people think about issues of the day'. Four of the five cities share another two items in common, (a), 'I find the radio good company', and (k), 'It keeps me up to date with current affairs'.

Interestingly, the items most frequently endorsed for local radio indicate two areas of gratification to be found in almost every uses and gratifications study of radio and television — informational or 'surveillance' satisfactions, and the more affectively termed satisfactions of mood control and companionship. We, the public, can, if we choose, use mass media to inform us about events past, present and future, and we can strike up a particular kind of companionly and knowing relationship with performers in the mass media. (This latter, very important, relational aspect of media use, sometimes called 'para-social interaction', is returned to frequently below.) We can also use media in order to help to manage our moods or feelings (to cheer us up, excite us, relax us, encourage nostalgia, and generally exercise our feelings).

Perhaps some readers are now experiencing confusion. How can local radio help people 'keep up with current affairs'? and what does 'keep me in touch with what is going on' mean? Since the uses and gratifications approach is concerned with subjective audience experience, we must accept that at core these statements can have as many meanings, or shades of meaning, as there are people who understand or relate to them; the reader will be familiar with the, 'Is the red I see the same red that you see?' argument.

At a slightly higher level of generality, if a statement is applied to a particular medium, then it will tend to take some of its objective meaning from that medium. For example, statement (e), 'keeps me in touch', could be applied by different (or the same) people to a specialist magazine on bee keeping and to an industrial 'house magazine'. The objective meaning is shaped by the medium to which the statement is applied. This poses the question: Does 'current affairs' mean the same thing when item (k) is applied to R4 as when it is applied to local radio? And the answer is that we don't really know but we can speculate. Both media broadcast national news and current affairs magazines; in fact in some instances a local radio station 'opts in' for the R4 national news and, for example, *The World at One*.

Local radio also broadcasts its own local news, and, significantly, examines the implications of national news for the locality. Searching for, and finding, the 'local angle' on a national story helps the recipient to relate to an event which might otherwise be just so many irrelevant 'newswords'. (Studies around the world show that a high proportion of broadcast news is registered and immediately forgotten by the audience.) This type of speculation indicates some of the varying shades of meaning that can be found in simple gratification statements, whilst also suggesting that the fact that local radio appears to do so well on current affairs, especially when compared with R4, is, with a little thought, comprehensible.

Another query about the table as a whole is a vehicle that can take us deeper into the uses and gratifications approach: Why do the satisfactions associated with national channels vary from city to city? Since R1 is the same in Liverpool and Bristol why does it get a 16 per cent endorsement as 'good company' in Liverpool and a 36 per cent endorsement in Bristol? Several reasons can be offered, the more straightforward ones first.

The two cities are here represented by samples designed to mirror the inhabitants of each city, and a quick look at section 1 of the results shows that even on basic demographic measures such as age and social class the samples are quite dissimilar. Perhaps if identical samples were drawn from the two cities then the differences would have decreased. Additionally, the values of the cities, their proximity to London, similarity between inhabitants and R1 presenters, and so on, all differ. These factors in themselves might explain city differences in the application of gratification statements to nationally available broadcasts, but there is more.

Earlier reference was made to the term 'functional orientation to media', which is a shorthand way of describing the overall pattern of gratifications that the individual attains from all available media. Such patterns are assumed when we refer to someone as a book man, or a POB (an Americanism standing for Print Oriented Bastard). Some of us 'get everything I want from the television', others 'couldn't do without a morning paper', most seek, or choose, a balance. Putting on one side the psychological and sociological determinants of this 'functional orientation', it is clear that another set of factors are at work and these can be summarised in the term, 'communications environment'. What channels of communication are open to the individual? And, after all this jargon, it is a very simple point that is being made — how people relate, in terms of gratification, to a given medium is influenced by the number and characteristics of alternative media available to them.

Returning to Bristol and Liverpool, it is obvious that the 'communications environments' of these two cities are quite different. Of particular relevance to this example is the location in Liverpool of Radio City, a twenty-four hour ILR. And a more detailed comparison of the two communications environments would throw up many other differences including: different BBC local radio stations, availability of local and regional newspapers, distribution of 'discos', nightclubs, book and record shops, and so on; the concept of a communications environment can be spread thin. [10]

By now it is clear that interpretation of uses and gratifications evidence is neither neat nor tidy. Some readers may find this irksome. So be it.

The general conclusions to be drawn from Table 6.27 are quite clearly favourable to local radio. In the context of city listening, local radio can at the very least hold its own against the national services. And the policy of mixed programming is associated with a wider range of salient satisfactions than is the case for the more limited content of an all-music station such as Radio One. In fact, within the sampling constraints of this study, it seems that local radio is rather successful at supplying the kinds of satisfaction that are associated with listening as such. But how does local radio fare as a specifically local medium catering to local communication needs? Several reasons have been offered for local radio's performance in the context of radio listening, but they carry little weight in the second context, that of local communications.

6. LOCAL COMMUNICATIONS AND ASSOCIATED USES AND GRATIFICATIONS

It is said that there are many ways of killing a cat, and the author has no reason to doubt the truth of this statement. There are also an increasing number of tried and tested ways of measuring a gratification. In this section we present two different measures of local communications gratifications, plus a summary measure based on the more rigorous technique.

The first measure is based on a shortish question (Q. 39) located towards the end of the questionnaire. Five local gratification statements were related by respondents to three local media: radio, press and television. For each statement the interviewee gave his or her opinion as to which medium was most suited to that satisfaction, which was second, and, by implication, which was least successful in providing that satisfaction. Interviewers were instructed not to take 'equal' for an answer, the individual was pushed to discriminate between the three local media. In order to make the implications of the resulting data as clear as possible, and to avoid catastrophic overloading of this section with numbers, the tables show first choices only.

Table 6.28 is in five parts, one for each gratification statement, and each figure given is the percentage of the whole sample nominating a particular medium as 'best' for the specified gratification.

Table 6.28 (a)
Local News and Information

'If you had to choose just one way of getting your local news and information, which would it be?'

	Local Radio	Local Newspaper	Local TV Programme
Oxford	32	54	15
Hull	25	54	21
Liverpool	27	44	29
Bristol	47	37	29
Nottingham	47	37	29

Taking Hull as an explanatory example, the table reads as follows. 25 per cent of the Hull sample nominated local radio as the best source of local news and information, 54 per cent nominated local press and 21 per cent local television programmes. Oxford shows a similar pattern, with the press gaining a major proportion of nominations followed by local radio and then local television programmes. Liverpool is also rather similar, although the television and radio percentage nominations are more or less alike. But Bristol and Nottingham show their own distinctive patterns, television dominating in Bristol and radio in Nottingham.

This is an opportune moment to remind the reader of the concept of 'communications environment'. Only in Bristol does television gain more than 29 per cent nomination, and Bristol is the only city in our sample which has its own regional television studio, at least in the sense that a regional news programme is regularly produced in Bristol, though of course other cities do have the facility to insert items into their regional news programmes. This line of analysis could be taken further by considering other ways in which inter-city variation in the table can be associated with variations in the five communications environments. But in interpreting differences between cities we must keep in mind the fact that the samples are not identical but matched to each city. Therefore a particular difference may be due not to, say, the excellence of 'The X Post', but to the relatively high percentage of middle class ladies in the city of X.

Table 6.28 (b)
Shopping News

'What about shopping news? Which is best for letting you know about good buys in the shops?'

	Local Radio	Local Newspaper	Local TV Programme
Oxford	26	63	11
Hull	6	86	8
Liverpool	11	70	20
Bristol	14	67	19
Nottingham	35	60	5

In this table there is no way of avoiding the fact that for shopping news local press reigns supreme. Interestingly there is no indication that the availability of commercial radio influences this finding unless the novelty of Radio Trent has given Nottingham that higher percentage for radio than recorded in any other city. The item's wording is clear enough and one can only point to the weight of local advertising carried in local daily/weekly press, and, perhaps, the advertising freesheets that are delivered to many households.

Table 6.28 (c)
Generates Pride in City

'Which one gives you a feeling of pride in (CITY)?'

	Local Radio	Local Newspaper	Local TV programme
Oxford	38	53	9
Hull	22	59	20
Liverpool	27	47	26
Bristol	14	39	48
Nottingham	45	41	13

Although local radio does relatively well in all cities, it is, as for local news, only in Bristol and Nottingham that the supremacy of the local press is challenged, by television and radio respectively.

Table 6.28 (d)
Future Events

'Which is best for letting you know about future events in the city?'

	Local Radio	Local Newspaper	Local TV programme
Oxford	45	49	6
Hull	34	62	4
Liverpool	26	57	18
Bristol	17	57	26
Nottingham	48	48	4

And, finally,

Table 6.28 (e)
Realistic Portrayal

'And which one portrays (CITY) as it really is?'

	Local Radio	Local Newspaper	Local TV programme
Oxford	34	59	7
Hull	23	72	5
Liverpool	24	55	21
Bristol	14	54	21
Nottingham	41	51	8

Before attempting to extract further meaning from these tables, some thought should be given to the way they were generated. They represent forced-choice answers to hypothetical questions and therefore have a certain measure of artificiality. The reality is that members of our samples do not have to pick just one medium. In daily life there is no call for them to decide 'which is best'; they can pick and choose everything, or nothing, according to how the mood takes them. Because of the artificiality of these questions they provoked an above average drop-out rate — some people found them impossible to answer and insisted upon picking two 'bests', but since drop-out never exceeded 20 per cent we can consider the results to be relatively representative.

Bearing in mind, then, the hypothetical nature of the questions upon which these results are based, what do they tell us about local gratifications? Firstly, it is apparent that in this forced-choice situation, and for the specified gratifications and uses, local press dominates. This is predictable to some extent by the exposure figures quoted earlier, for in general more people use local newspapers than local radio. Television, in the form of local news magazines, has a far wider editorial area than either press or local radio, it is not surprising that it fails to achieve the same level of nomination as the other media for these local uses.

The tables show some recurrent patterns for individual cities, of which perhaps the most obvious is the tendency for local radio in Nottingham to gain as many or more nominations than the local press there. Tables in section 2 showed that Oxford had the smallest readership, followed by Nottingham, and yet the percentage nominating local press as best for each satisfaction is consistently higher in Oxford than in Nottingham. This suggests that radio's performance in those samples is not just a reflection of low readership. On the other hand, Hull recorded rather higher listening to Radio Humberside than did Nottingham for Radio Nottingham, and yet Humberside never challenges the *Hull Daily Mail* in this hypothetical question. One answer to this problem arising from Nottingham's idiosyncracy takes account of the newly opened (at the time of the survey) ILR station in Nottingham — Radio Trent. The introduction of a new medium can precipitate a general reorganisation of individuals' functional orientations to media,[11] and the newest medium may for a while be favoured by a novelty effect as well as high expectations. Over time, however, the novelty effect is likely to wear off, with exposure falling into a steady pattern and expectations becoming translated into more realistic assessments.

Yet more meaning can be extracted from the data if the tables are re-expressed in terms of profiles for the two dominant media. Rather than asking which medium is most successful, we can look to the relative success of each medium across the five gratification statements. Table 6.29 does just that and shows the rank order of gratifications for radio and press in the five cities.

Table 6.29
Rankings of Five Gratifications for Local Radio and Local Press

Items	Oxford LR	LP	Hull LR	LP	Liverpool LR	LP	Bristol LR	LP	Nottingham LR	LP
(a) Local news and information	4	3	2	4	1	5	2	5	2	5
(b) Shopping news	5	1	5	1	5	1	3	1	5	1
(c) Pride in city	2	4	4	5	1	4	3	4	3	4
(d) Future events	1	4	1	3	3	2	1	2	1	3
(e) Realistic portrayal	3	2	3	2	4	3	3	3	4	2

The table shows that the rank order of gratifications for Radio Oxford is: a-4th, b-5th, c-2nd, d-1st, and, e-3rd. It is in the nature of this table's construction that press and radio could have the same rank profiles, but this is not the case. Indeed, there is some indication across cities of the two media carving up and sharing out gratifications. To put it another way, by asking a forced, hypothetical question we begin to see how one medium is best suited to one particular range of gratifications, another to another. For all five cities item (b), good for shopping news, is ranked first for press, last for radio. Radio, on the other hand, tends to rank higher for local news than does press. And, except for Liverpool and Oxford, item (c), generation of pride in city, falls in the lower portion of ranks for both press and radio, but there is some suggestion that radio may be more suited to this type of satisfaction than is the press. The reverse seems to apply to item (e), realistic portrayal of city, with a tendency for this quality to feature higher for the press than for radio. It is tempting to speculate that these two satisfactions are mutually exclusive, but these findings do not justify such an assumption.

The predominance of the local press as a source of shopping news has already been referred to along with the suggestion that this is a function of its high advertising content. Conversely local radio, whilst occasionally featuring 'consumer concerns' and giving market reports, typically has little to say about, for instance, wallpaper/carpet/clothing sales. We might intepret this result, then, as being related to the content of the media rather than to any other characteristic of the medium as such.

'Future events', on the other hand, shows a tendency to reverse the 'shopping news' finding. Local radio has earned a reputation as a provider of information about 'What's on'. Again this might be seen as a consequence of medium content and the policy of local radio to allow, as it were, free advertising to local groups. Thus a picture of the week's events emerges from radio, one that is far more detailed than that provided by the press which, by and large, is dependent upon organisations buying space in the local newspaper. Interestingly, a reversal might have occurred if the question had been phrased, 'tells you about past events'. Local weekly newspapers, in particular, tend to report on some events after they have occurred; a whist drive or garden party which has been publicised on local radio will (not necessarily as a consequence of this publicity) be reported by the local press. This suggests one way in which the complex relationships between media operate. A radio broadcast might lead the individual to attend some function, and the act of attending then increases interest in reading about the function in the local weekly. The link is unlikely to be strong enough to encourage the individual to buy the paper, but it may well influence what he or she chooses to read in the paper. In this sense media are interdependent and together form the 'communications environment'.

Presenting the information generated by Q. 39 in two different forms demonstrates how more than one set of meanings, or levels of meaning, can be elicited from the same basic data. In this case both treatments are quite admissible but could have different practical implications for the operators of local media. And to the researcher this type of manipulation is essential to the process of producing models of reality; almost every table of data can be turned inside out, or made to stand on its head, and each time the table is re-expressed some new shade of meaning or fresh hypothesis may be suggested.

Question 39, being forced-choice, tended to emphasise differences between media — perhaps artificially so. Is it the case that different media provide different satisfactions, that radio complements the press? The main part of this section on gratifications and local media is based upon questions that did not impose forced comparisons and therefore more nearly approximated daily media use. Up to seven individual local media were rated for their tendency to provide thirteen listed satisfactions. Before administering each set of ratings, interviewers checked whether the question was appropriate to the respondent and only those who regularly used the medium in question were included. The thirteen items were based on qualitative group work. The aim was to produce a list of satisfactions that could be equally well applied to the three media (press, radio, television). Thus, items were omitted that might relate to special features of one medium but could not be meaningfully applied to others. Because of this approach, which is in a sense comparative, certain satisfactions that are important to the individual are ignored, for example, those associated with Births, Deaths and Marriages, an ever popular component of local press (and the focus for a splendid gratification study in its own right). The inventory also denied the possibility to express special satisfaction in local radio's provision of locally produced music, and 'swop shop' programmes.

Only one item proved too difficult to phrase in such a way that it could be applied across the board and so this was reworded from 'The people on . . . have become like friends to me' for radio and television, to 'I feel as if I know some of the contributors', for local press. Group discussions suggested that in its original wording this satisfaction had no clear counterpart in the local press, but the item was included in order to produce a better balance.

Different availabilities of local morning and local weekly

71

newspapers, and the small recorded readerships, justify devoting the remainder of this section to the three major local media. Independent Local Radio is also omitted since only in Liverpool was there a station that had existed for longer than a month at the time of fieldwork.

A standard introduction to the question was read to each respondent:

> Here are some statements about local broadcasting. Tell me after each one how you feel about it by using an item on this card (CARD B: READ THROUGH THE SCALE). Here's the first statement: *BBC Look North* (the programme was named and preceded by BBC or ITV) makes me feel like part of a real community. Use one of the items on your card to tell me how you feel about that, do you agree strongly, agree, have no opinion or feel uncertain, disagree.

Interviewers reported no difficulty with these questions, sample members soon 'caught on', and the interviewer maintained a steady pace, since what was wanted was first reactions rather than detailed and considered opinions. At this stage it is sufficient to show the results of these questions by reporting the percentages of informants who responded Agree Strongly, or Agree, though a more exhaustive use of the data is to follow.

The percentages in Table 6.30, which is a long running table interspersed with text passages, refer to the proportion of all respondents for each city who agree with a particular statement: they thus indicate the satisfactions associated with particular media for the city as a whole. This point is taken up later when some findings are re-expressed as percentages of listeners, readers or viewers. Table 6.30 indicates percentages of each city sample who agree, or agree strongly, with the linking of the gratification statement, ' . . . makes me feel like part of a real community' with the nominated local media.

Table 6.30 (a)
. . . Makes Me Feel Like Part of a Real Community

Medium	Oxford	Hull	Liverpool	Bristol	Nottingham
BBC LR	37 (50)	51 (32)	34 (48)	27 (64)	42 (34)
BBC TV	26 (51)	17 (57)	28 (44)	37 (36)	15 (62)
ITV	26 (58)	44 (34)	42 (34)	32 (48)	27 (40)

Medium	Oxford	Hull	Liverpool	Bristol	Nottingham
Local evening	40 (42)	56 (11)	45 (30)	36 (32)	34 (36)

This table is more complex than its followers in order to ensure that the reader takes account of different levels of exposure between media and cities. Unbracketed numbers refer to the percentage of respondents who agreed with the statement, while bracketed numbers are the percentages of the whole sample who — because of infrequent exposure to the medium in question — were not asked to complete this question. Oxford is used as a working example. 37 per cent agreed that Radio Oxford made them feel part of a real community, a further 50 per cent were not asked the question. For BBC TV regional news programmes, 26 per cent agreed, and 51 per cent did not receive the question. Bracketed numbers would be the same for each segment of Table 6.30 and are only included in Table 6.30 (a). The implications are important, since it is with their help that we can explore how well the medium satisfies its audience and how well the medium satisfies the community.

Spelling out the actual implications, we find that for 'community' Radio Oxford gained 37 per cent of the whole sample (200), i.e. 74 actual informants (37 per cent of 200) agreed with the statements, but only 100 informants claimed to be listeners, so 74 per cent of listeners agreed with the statement. Since the 50 per cent listening figure in Oxford might confuse the principle being applied, another example is worked through. Bristol for radio and press shows 27 per cent and 36 per cent agreement respectively. Therefore, the actual number of individuals agreeing was 54 and 72, respectively (27 per cent and 36 per cent of 200 re-expressed as raw figures), but 64 per cent did not receive the question for radio, which means that only 72 (200-2x64) individuals were asked about local radio and 'community'. Therefore 75 per cent (54 as a percentage of 72) of listeners agreed with the statement. Readers formed 68 per cent of the sample, (100 minus 32) which is 136 informants, of whom 72 agreed with the link between 'community' and local press, i.e., 53 per cent (72 as a percentage of 136). Again, Radio Bristol -- 27 per cent of sample, or 75 per cent of listeners: Bristol local evening paper = 36 per cent of sample, or 53 per cent of readers. Because of different audience sizes, the medium that 'contributes' most to its audience need not 'contribute' most to the community — and vice versa.

And now, back to the table, which will be dealt with in terms of contribution to the community. Unlike Table 6.29, which presented forced-choice data, Table 6.30 could result from people agreeing with everything, that is to say that an individual could agree that both media made him or her 'feel part of a real community'. Even so we again note a tendency for local press to dominate, although this tendency is less marked than in the earlier table. Again, also, we find Nottingham and Bristol deviating from the pattern. Another factor which arises from this part of Table 6.30 and can be applied to the remainder of the table, is the extent to which each city, as represented by our samples, achieves a particular satisfaction from the communications environment. In the case of 'makes me feel like part of a real community', there is apparently more chance that this feeling is applicable to the media in Hull than in Bristol. There are several possible explanations for this, and considering one or two of them at this stage will help to familiarise the reader a little more with the undergrowth of uses and gratifications evidence. The answer could depend on the media, the audience, or the city. Perhaps Bristol media are simple less successful at broadcasting content which, other things being equal, would encourage a sense of community. Or maybe the audience feels no desire for the sense of community, or again, they might already have it in abundance — in either case they would not feature this gratification in their 'functional orientation' to local media. Finally, it could be the case that the city itself, the built and social environment, is such that it discourages, or makes redundant, any feelings of community. In fact, of course, common sense tells us that some combination of medium, audience, and city-based factors is at work in producing these kinds of results. 'Uses and gratifications' primarily concerns adaptation: the individual adapts that which is outside him- or herself (including mass and local media) to his or her own experienced requirements — and with greater or lesser degrees of success.

This basic assertion helps to place the uses and gratifications approach to the media in its correct perspective. The satisfactions found in media use are usually to be found elsewhere: in the clothes we wear, the food we eat, the shops we use, our affiliations to political and social groups, our participation in sports and other leisure pursuits and, perhaps most importantly, in our relationships with other people. Indeed, some theoreticians[12] have argued that media-based satisfactions are always 'functional alternatives' — second bests, substitutes for the real thing. As evidence they point to the greater use of mass media by those who have limited resources than by those who are better supplied with a range of social opportunities. Certainly it is the case that any study of the uses and gratifications associated with mass media (or, of course, local media) must remain incomplete by failing to take account of those other alternatives. The lines drawn around the investigation, although necessary and productive, are also imaginary, the 'communications environment' is but one sequence of threads in 'life's rich tapestry'.

Returning to Table 6.30, which is now allowed to run, the reader should bear in mind that crisply printed tables often convey a spurious air of definitive confidence. There is nothing sacred or immutable about 49 per cent, it simply means that approximately half of the people interviewed in Oxford agreed that Radio Oxford 'is a good way for me to find out what is going on in and around Oxford'.

Table 6.30 (b)
' . . . is a Good Way for Me to Find Out What is Going On
In and Around . . . '

	Oxford	Hull	Liverpool	Bristol	Nottingham
BBC LR	49	65	45	34	64
BBC TV	22	24	42	59	17
ITV	23	58	53	46	25
Local evening	55	82	66	63	60

(c) I sometimes talk about things I've heard/seen/read . . .

	Oxford	Hull	Liverpool	Bristol	Nottingham
BBC LR	45	61	41	33	58
BBC TV	40	33	47	59	34
ITV	35	61	57	48	56
Local evening	54	84	64	62	58

(d) I find the local weather and road reports useful

	Oxford	Hull	Liverpool	Bristol	Nottingham
BBC LR	44	48	37	28	46
BBC TV	33	26	34	51	26
ITV	26	46	45	36	43

	Oxford	Hull	Liverpool	Bristol	Nottingham
(d)					
Local evening	36	45	41	33	40

(e) It keeps me in touch with people and places I know.

BBC LR	40	48	32	32	50
BBC TV	22	24	30	48	19
ITV	24	45	42	38	28
Local evening	40	67	53	55	48

(f) . . . shows me what ordinary people in (CITY) are thinking and talking.

BBC LR	42	60	38	30	56
BBC TV	18	19	37	50	15
ITV	18	48	48	42	25
Local evening	46	73	55	55	50

(g) . . . keeps me well informed about local sports.

BBC LR	40	48	39	28	38
BBC TV	14	16	28	40	13
ITV	18	38	37	36	28
Local evening	44	62	53	47	41

(h) The people on . . . have become like friends to me, or, I feel as if I know some of the contributors.

BBC LR	22	30	20	20	26
BBC TV	20	12	19	26	11
ITV	16	20	29	32	16

	Oxford	Hull	Liverpool	Bristol	Nottingham
(h)					
Local evening	26	26	22	22	22

(i) It reminds me what the city was like in earlier days

	Oxford	Hull	Liverpool	Bristol	Nottingham
BBC LR	24	26	13	20	35
BBC TV	11	8	14	32	8
ITV	10	22	18	30	14
Local evening	31	42	31	40	38

(j) . . . stands up for things I believe in.

	Oxford	Hull	Liverpool	Bristol	Nottingham
BBC LR	20	34	17	18	21
BBC TV	17	14	17	27	8
ITV	14	32	25	27	10
Local evening	18	32	27	27	23

(k) It tells me about developments in (CITY), new buildings, roads, that sort of thing.

	Oxford	Hull	Liverpool	Bristol	Nottingham
BBC LR	45	51	39	30	44
BBC TV	20	21	40	55	20
ITV	24	47	49	43	39
Local evening	55	74	65	63	61

(l) It gives an interesting local slant on national news stories.

	Oxford	Hull	Liverpool	Bristol	Nottingham
BBC LR	43	62	41	32	52
BBC TV	28	32	44	54	28
ITV	28	62	54	46	46
Local evening	45	70	59	58	51

(m) Are there any people on . . . that you really look forward to seeing/hearing?

(percentage naming a performer)

	Oxford	Hull	Liverpool	Bristol	Nottingham
BBC LR	14	15	13	6	15
BBC TV	12	7	15	12	8
ITV	12	25	28	24	10

The material is lengthy and detailed and to restate its content in text is an unnecessary imposition on reader and writer alike, but both can use Table 6.30 as a resource to turn back to when needed. For the present we will attempt to extract some overall patterns which might illuminate the concepts of communications environment and functional orientation.

Looking through the table a sense of consistency is found and the reader will doubtless spot several patterns and trends. A useful technique for revealing trends is the very simple exercise familiar from earlier tables — extracting the 'top five'. In this case the top five shows us not which medium is best at providing satisfactions but which satisfactions each medium most frequently provides (or provides to the largest proportion of the community). It is clear that for the majority of cities and the majority of satisfactions the local evening paper is, as suggested by the earlier measure, making the greatest overall contribution. Table 6.31 allows us to delve below this pattern and concern ourselves with intra-media comparisons as well as inter-media comparisons. The twelve gratification statements (item (m) is excluded since it cannot reasonably be applied to print) are listed for each medium (in each city), and the top five uses are shown, that is, those items which gain highest percentage agreement for each medium.

The table is clarified by taking Oxford as an example. Media are indicated by capital letters: R — Local Radio. B — BBC TV, I — Independent Television, and P — Local Evening Paper. Thus, for Oxford, item (a), 'makes me feel like part of a real community', is amongst the top five most highly endorsed items for both BBC and ITV, while only Radio Humberside features this satisfaction amongst its top five. Two satisfactions are common to all four media in all five cities, namely: (c), 'I sometimes talk about things I've heard/seen/read . . . ', and (l), 'It gives me an interesting local slant on national news stories'. Radio is consistent across cities for (c), (l), and (b), ' . . . is a good way for me to find out what is going on in and around . . . '. Both ITV and local press are consistent on (k), 'It tells me about developments . . . ', and local press is consistent on (b), 'What's going

78

on' and (f), ' . . . shows me what ordinary people in (city) are talking and thinking about'. Finally, BBC TV regional news magazines consistently include road and weather reports (d) amongst their top fives.

Table 6.31
Top Fives for Local Media in Each City

Gratification statements	Oxford	Hull	Liverpool	Bristol	Nottingham
(a) . . . makes me feel like part of a real community	B I	R			
(b) . . . is a good way for me to find out what is going on in and around . . .	R B	P R B I P	R B I P	R B I P	R I P
(c) I sometimes talk about things I've heard/seen/ read . . .	R B I P	R B I P	R B I P	R B I P	R B I P
(d) I find the local weather and road reports useful	R B I	B	B	B	B
(e) It keeps me in touch with people and places I know	B I	B		P	R B
(f) . . . shows me what ordinary people in (city) are thinking and talking about	P R	I P	R I P	R I P	R I P
(g) . . . keeps me well informed about local sports					

	Oxford	Hull	Liverpool	Bristol	Nottingham
(h) The people on . . . have become like friends to me, or, I feel as if I know some of the contributors					
(i) It reminds me what the city was like in earlier days					
(j) . . . stands up for things I believe in					
(k) It tells me about developments in (city), new buildings, roads, that sort of thing	R I P	R I P	R B I P	R B I P	B I P
(l) It gives an interesting local slant on national news stories	R B I P	R B I P	R B I P	R B I P	R B I P

The degree of patterning clearly undermines any assumption that the instrument as a whole was generating 'random noise' or indeed measuring 'noise in the system' due to random guessing on the part of respondents. Had that been the case, Table 6.31 would have been littered with capital letters. A noteworthy element of this patterning is the white rectangle caused by the omission of four items from all top fives. The lower performance items are: (g) '. . . keeps me well informed about local sports', (h) 'The people on . . . have become like friends to me', (i) 'It reminds me of what the city was like in earlier days', and (j) '. . . stands up for things I believe in'.

If, for a moment, we ignore which medium is contributing in order to isolate cities that do not feature a particular item at all, an extremely high degree of inter-city consistency clearly emerges. Only two items are inconsistent, (a) 'feeling of community' features in

Oxford and Hull but nowhere else, and, perhaps significantly, Liverpool not only omits 'feeling of community', but also excludes (e) 'It keeps me in touch with people and places I know'. (This tendency for Liverpool to be idiosyncratic has already been noted, and again it is clear that the deviation is in line with a richly interconnected community. Is the Liverpudlian so 'well connected' that he or she has no need of 'functional alternatives' provided by media in order to keep in touch, and have a feeling of 'real' community?)

Whereas Table 6.27, based on forced choices, seemed to suggest some rudimentary sharing out of satisfactions between radio and print, this table indicates a higher degree of overlap. In part at least this difference can be explained by reference to differences between the two samples involved. Indeed, two items appear in the top five of every medium in every city, they are (c) 'I sometimes talk about things I've seen/heard/read . . .' and (l) 'It gives an interesting local slant on national news stories'. Although, as suggested earlier, it would have been possible to include other gratification statements which were specific to particular media, and might, therefore, have appeared in particular top fives, it is unlikely, to say the least, that any one of them would have appeared alongside (c) and (l) in all top fives.

In a sense, then, these two satisfactions are core local communications. As such, they are worthy of some comment and will be returned to later, but for the present it is interesting to note that whilst one — local slant on national news — is a local gratification *par excellence,* the other — talk about — is a satisfaction (or use) which emerges in almost every uses and gratifications study ever undertaken. It plays some part in audience usage, roughly speaking, for all media in all countries — for children and adults. Indeed this satisfaction has been accorded its own metaphorical label — 'coin of exchange'. The coin of exchange tag emphasises a use of media content in social transactions, or conversations (transaction is a rather more accurate description since it applies to a wider range of verbal communication than does 'conversation').

In a national context (in fact, even in certain international contexts) the media provide common ground, shared experience, and thus, useful topics of conversation which help to initiate or maintain social relationships. At the national level this satisfaction is frequently related to fictional content — soap opera, Kojak and so on, but, in the absence of such content at a local level, we begin to see the validity of a 'parish pump' image of local media. Although the satisfaction is not given meaning here in terms of the type of content that is talked

81

about, it seems that a major topic of media-based conversation in this local context is likely to be local news, or the local implications of national news. This provides another clue to the community binding or building role of local media.

But the table as a whole also presents a challenge to the uses and gratifications approach — and this challenge should not be ignored. Put crudely, the table suggests that local media tend to be good at, and appreciated for, mainly the same things. There is little evidence here for the idea that each medium does what it does best, and that together they form a communications environment that is optimal in the sense of efficiently providing a wide range of satisfactions.

The challenge is no Aunt Sally. It would have been more than reasonable to expect Table 6.31 to show a quite different set of consistencies with radio accounting for one set of gratifications, the press another, and television a third; surely that would indicate a healthy communications environment? But rather than mutually exclusive specialisation we seem to have found evidence of a limiting competition. There are one or two provisos that weaken the challenge. Highly specialised content and related satisfactions are excluded, for example, Births, Deaths and Marriages (press), swop shops and religious programmes (radio), and televised interviews. And another argument is that the reported figures are artificial. Because a satisfaction does not occur in the top fives, it does not of necessity follow that the medium is not providing it. For example, inspection of Table 6.30 shows that some items appearing in, say, television top fives, do not appear in the top fives of the local press — but they are more frequently provided by local press. And, of course, as outlined in the discussion of 'listening gratifications', the items themselves take on certain shades of meaning from the media to which they are applied, and, therefore, complementarity is, to some extent, implicit to the table.

But these are nit-picking arguments that cannot successfully undermine the clear implication that whereas the forced-choice question conveyed a picture of complementarity, these data suggest that, on many matters of importance to citizens, the local media are providing a similar range of satisfactions.

The apparent contradiction between the two sets of results is probably best resolved in terms of differences of specificity between the local satisfactions involved. There are certain highly specific functions that one or another local medium is best suited to perform — the press to give shopping news, for example, and the radio to broadcast news of forthcoming events and entertainments. But when we enter a realm where more broadly conceived categories of local communication need are being served, there the radio, press and regional television seem mainly to be tuned in to the same wavelengths of expectation and satisfaction. It is as if, certain specific forms of service apart, the entire local communications complex is directed to virtually the same functions. On the other hand it is possible that different sections of the community seek satisfaction from different media. In the next section we ask: Who gets satisfaction from what?

7. SUMMARY SCORES OF
LOCAL SATISFACTIONS

Before taking a more detailed look at the audience it is necessary to explain how sample members' responses to a number of individual gratification statements were combined into a more summary measure. The reader will recall from a previous section of this report how certain opinion statements concerning urban amenities and feelings about the five cities were converted into simple scores which, in lay person's terms at least, could be said to measure civic attitudes. In order to facilitate further exploration of town dwellers' subjective reactions to the five communications environments, a similar form of scaling, or scoring, was applied to the local gratifications data.

Before attempting to prepare such scores an analysis was conducted which allowed the investigator to study the entrails of his gratification data. Responses to each item were related, statistically, to responses to every other item in order to ascertain how far the items were, or could be said to be, measuring the same thing. This analysis revealed that the items, taken together, were suited to the computation of 'total gratification' scores for each medium. The process was simple but lengthy. Each of the five ways of responding to a gratification item was re-scored so that 'Agree Strongly' became '2', 'Agree' became '1', and any other response was made equal to zero. (Several more complex conversions could have been used, but this, the simplest, proved adequate.) The computer then exhaustively searched its memory and, whenever it found an 'Agree Strongly' or 'Agree', allocated the appropriate score. It then calculated and memorised the total gratification score for each respondent on each medium. Finally, the computer was able to print out total and average gratification scores for any defined group of respondents. Averages in this context are general indicants of how a particular medium performs in providing satisfaction to the members of a defined group. [13] Table 6.32 presents the average scores for each medium and city, based on the frequency and intensity of agreement with the twelve local gratification statements.

Table 6.32
Total Gratifications, Averages for Media and Cities

Total gratification for:	Oxford	Hull	Liverpool	Bristol	Nottingham
BBC TV	3.5	2.8	4.1	6.5	2.4
ITV	3.4	6.5	6.4	5.5	4.1
BBC local radio	6.0	7.3	4.7	3.8	6.6
ILR	—	—	3.0	—	1.6
Local evening paper	6.1	8.4	6.5	6.5	6.2
Local weekly paper	3.1	0.4	3.1	0.3	0.4

The table is intriguing enough, but first a reminder of what the figures represent. Each figure is an average score on a scale of total gratification provided by a particular medium in a particular city. Furthermore, the figures are based upon frequency of agreement with gratifications statements and the intensity of such agreement. Previous tables have only taken account of frequency of agreement; bringing in intensity slightly alters the picture, for now we note that local radio is faring a little better in relation to local press than in earlier tables. Independent Local Radio averages are given for Nottingham and Liverpool; local morning newspaper figures are not reported since readership was minimal; local weekly papers are included for interest sake, even though it is clear that in three of the towns readership was again minimal.

Returning to the major local media — radio, local evening, and television — we can again search for consistencies. Briefly, for the main uses of these scores are yet to appear, in four out of the five cities the local evening paper emerges as a dominant source of satisfaction. The exception is Nottingham, where radio dominates, while in Oxford there is a negligible difference between radio and press. Except for Bristol and Liverpool, television makes the least pronounced contribution to overall satisfaction. Oddly, the BBC TV score is equal to that of the press in Bristol, and this finding links with a general indication that Bristol, whilst not by our measures having the highest percentage local radio audience, shows a distinctively favourable appreciation of the BBC.

In other cities it is clear that ITV is more finely tuned to the locality, a condition that applies particularly to Hull but also in Nottingham and Liverpool. The difference between ITV and BBC TV in Oxford is negligible, but the relatively low contribution of TV as a whole to local communication needs in Oxford is consistent with sustained grumbling in the Oxford group discussions. A number of group members felt it necessary to complain that both the BBC and ITV regarded Oxford as little more than an area of overlap between Birmingham and London.

Another way of looking at this table is afforded by the perspective of a local communications environment. It is quite clear that whilst average scores on some media fluctuate from city to city, the local evening press gains a consistently high average score, the only deviation from a row of sixes being Hull with the extremely high average score of 8.4. Local radio shows a tendency for the largest cities to gain the lowest average scores, and earlier comments about Nottingham are reflected in the fact that Radio Nottingham secured a higher average than did Nottingham's local press. Although both ITV and BBC TV vary from city to city, BBC TV shows greater variation with average gratification scores ranging from 2.8 (Hull) to 6.5 (Bristol). If we average the two television scores (a dubious procedure, but, as Saki noted, 'A little inaccuracy sometimes saves a ton of explanation') it is interesting to note that inhabitants of the two largest cities, Liverpool and Bristol, registered the highest average amounts of gratification from television. Within the limitations set by our samples and methods, it appears that, to use a manufactured quotation, 'there is more satisfaction floating around in Hull than in Oxford'. It is possible, though mathematically inadvisable, to add together the four averages for the major local media in each city, which would then be a rough (and dubious) indicant of the overall satisfaction provided by the five different communications environments. Out of devilish disregard for mathematical niceties, however, the author has added these averages — just to see how they look: Oxford — 19, Hull — 25, Liverpool — 22, Bristol — 22, and Nottingham — 19. They are, of course, amazingly crude 'fun' figures that take no account of a myriad of inter-city differences.

Now it is time to enter the very heart of uses and gratifications data, leave the gross patterns and begin to consider defined groups of people and how they have fared in their search for satisfaction. But first, where are we, and how did we get here? The first set of results presented featured sample characteristics in terms of basic demographic background and a number of measures that might be expected to relate to local communications, for example, feelings about the locality, proportion of friends and kin who live in the locality and so on. Next we considered exposure to local media, and then surface assessments of radio and newspaper content. Moving deeper into the experience of using media, via images of local radio, we tackled the question of how well local radio fares in the context of radio listening *per se.* Finally, we presented and commented on local communications gratifications and, in order to allow a more incisive analysis, calculated total gratification scores. Section 8 uses these scores in an attempt to highlight background characteristics that are related to the provision of local gratifications by local media.

8. AUDIENCE CHARACTERISTICS THAT ARE ASSOCIATED WITH LOCAL COMMUNICATIONS SATISFACTIONS

By now it will be obvious that, even with the relatively straightforward approach adopted in this report, a vast amount of information has been secured, and that in reporting our findings we are being selective. Several highly sophisticated techniques are available to analyse the relationships that exist between individual characteristics and media-based gratification, but here a relatively robust, common sense analysis has been used. Even so, there is a danger that we might become bogged down in detail, especially in this section where we consider a variety of background influences on local communication satisfactions. To avoid this danger, we concern ourselves with the two local media which are most committedly local — radio and the local evening paper. Television, it can be argued, tends to transmit only 30 minutes, or thereabouts, of local broadcasting a day. And even this is more properly described as regional. Furthermore, the use of television as a source of local gratifications is likely to be heavily influenced by other factors that are unrelated to its local content. Of course this is, as ever, swings and roundabouts country. By sharpening the focus on local communication in this way, we lose some of the benefits of a broader perspective on the local communications environment.

We have at our disposal certain summarising measures of the total gratifications provided by local media. These measures are based on both frequency and intensity of agreement with specific gratification statements. As in the preceding table we will base our explorations on average scores on these summarising scales, considering each of several background characteristics in turn and moving from the most straightforward to the more complex. Table 6.33 presents the results of calculating average gratification scores for men and women which are based upon full samples and therefore represent cities (actual, plus potential, audience) rather than readers and listeners only.

Taking local radio first, it is clear that little difference between the sexes occurs in Oxford (5.9 − 6.0), Liverpool (4.8 − 4.5) and Nottingham (6.4 − 6.7). In Bristol and Hull, however, there is a marked tendency for women to gain greater overall satisfaction from local radio than men. Local press scores reflect little difference between the sexes in Hull, Liverpool and Bristol, but in both the Oxford and Nottingham samples there is a marked and similar difference with men gaining higher average satisfaction from the local evening paper than women. Comparing the two media, the overall

Table 6.33
Average Gratification Scores x Sex x Media x City

	Oxford		Hull		Liverpool		Bristol		Nottingham	
	Local Radio	Local Press	Local Radio	Local Press	Local Radio	Local Press	Local Radio	Local Press	Local Radio	Local Press
Male	5.9	7.1	6.7	8.3	4.8	6.4	3.4	6.5	6.4	7.7
Female	6.0	5.2	7.9	8.5	4.5	6.7	4.3	6.5	6.7	4.9

Table 6.34
Average Gratification Scores x Social Class x Media x City

	Oxford		Hull		Liverpool		Bristol		Nottingham	
	Local Radio	Local Press	Local Radio	Local Press	Local Radio	Local Press	Local Radio	Local Press	Local Radio	Local Press
Middle (ABC1)	4.3	3.7	5.4	8.6	3.1	4.0	3.0	6.9	5.1	5.3
Working (C2DE)	7.2	8.0	8.1	7.8	5.1	6.6	4.3	6.3	6.8	6.6

pattern of press superiority still prevails, with the exception of women in Oxford and Nottingham, where BBC local radio provides greater gratification than the local newspaper. In the table as a whole, there is also some support for the hypothesis that in seeking local communication satisfaction, men are relatively more press oriented than women. That is, in four of the five cities (excluding Liverpool), the difference between press and radio scores favouring local newspapers is greater for the male than the female respondents.

As Table 6.34 shows, a splitting of the samples by social grade reveals marked differences by class in overall gratifications obtained from the two local media. In every city the C2DE group gained higher average gratification scores from BBC local radio than did their middle class counterparts. The same pattern obtained for local press use in three cities — Oxford, Liverpool and Nottingham. In Bristol there was some indication that middle class Bristolians gained more from the local press than did working class Bristolians, and the same applied to the people of Hull. This, then, is an extremely consistent table suggesting that local media tend to be more rewardingly used by working class than middle class citizens. The finding is consistent with common sense and earlier research.

The middle classes are more mobile; ever striving, they are more likely to follow a graded career structure and move around the country; accordingly, as a class, they are less 'local'. That the difference is most marked in Oxford, and reversed in Hull and Bristol (for the press) is a little more difficult to explain, but we might speculate that Hull and Bristol share, for different reasons, a higher degree of self-sufficiency than do the other cities. Hull is a 'back of beyond' city, which must generate its own leisure/political concerns with little regard to any nearby big brother conurbations. Liverpool is an aggressive working class parish. Bristol . . . perhaps a middle class commune far enough from the London metropolis to have deliberately created its own thriving middle class culture. Oxford, on the other hand, is a Don's spit from London . . .

Romantically, then, it seems that these figures correspond with the notion of the working classes embedded in local communities, the middle classes and upwardly mobile chasing the bitch goddess — taking time off occasionally to moon over their lost roots: It is an idea so old that it has Weskers.

Taken in conjunction with Table 6.33, Table 6.35 suggests that a pattern of results may be beginning to emerge for the five cities. Specifically, there is an indication of some similarity between the results for Hull, Nottingham, and Bristol; it will be recalled that for these three cities local radio yielded higher mean gratification scores

90

Table 6.35
Average Gratification Scores x Age x Media x City

	Oxford Local Radio	Local Press	Hull Local Radio	Local Press	Liverpool Local Radio	Local Press	Bristol Local Radio	Local Press	Nottingham Local Radio	Local Press
18–35	6.0	5.9	3.7	6.6	5.0	6.5	1.6	6.0	5.5	3.4
36–55	5.7	6.7	7.7	8.7	5.5	7.0	3.9	6.7	5.3	6.5
56 +	6.2	6.0	10.6	9.9	3.5	5.0	5.5	6.7	8.5	8.2

Table 6.36
Average Gratification Scores x Place of Birth x Media x City

	Oxford Local Radio	Local Press	Hull Local Radio	Local Press	Liverpool Local Radio	Local Press	Bristol Local Radio	Local Press	Nottingham Local Radio	Local Press
City	7.4	6.9	7.5	8.9	5.0	7.2	4.0	7.4	6.6	6.8
'County'	8.9	8.3	8.1	7.6	3.5	4.4	4.1	5.2	8.6	5.6
Elsewhere	4.5	5.3	6.7	7.5	4.6	5.6	3.2	5.7	4.9	6.0

for women than men (although the difference was marginal in the case of Nottingham). And here again, when the role of age is considered, it is clear that these three cities present a similar profile. In each case the amount of satisfaction increases with age, Bristol being an exception in the case of local press. The Oxford and Liverpool results, on the other hand, seem to reveal a curved relationship between average gratification score and age, with the 36—55 year olds scoring higher for local press, and lower, in the case of Oxford, for local radio. The most dramatic findings depicted in this table are those for Hull and Bristol where the average gratification scores range from 3.7 to 10.6, and, 1.6 to 5.5, respectively.

Moving on to variables that were not predetermined by the Centre, (for the previous three tables were based upon quota distributions), the reader should bear in mind the search for patterns in the results. Although each table has its own particular interest, it is perhaps the emerging overall picture that is of greatest significance.

Table 6.36 shows how place of birth is related to gratification scores. Respondents were grouped into three categories, those born in the city, those born in the 'county', by which we mean a notional area around the city up to a maximum of fifty miles from its centre and where the nominated city is in fact a focal point, and, thirdly, 'elsewhere', that is, born in an area totally unrelated to the city.

Predictably, the third group of respondents tends to produce lower scores, but what is rather less predictable is a marked tendency for 'county' respondents to score higher than city respondents. For local radio this finding applies to all cities except Liverpool, and for local press the direction is reversed with city people scoring higher in all locations except Oxford. This is an interesting distinction between radio and press which is not easily explained. One possible explanation for the general finding, however, would suggest a different type of orientation for those who were born and are still living in the city from those who were born in the 'county' and moved into the city. Those with roots in the city may be more interested in a broader surveillance of what has happened to old acquaintances and areas they knew in childhood, whilst 'county' informants would tend to down-grade such information but, perhaps, gain more satisfaction from radio provided news of future events and developments. It is possible that the underlying dynamic is one which combines social integration with a degree of civic involvement. The inconsistency of Liverpool then links up with an earlier finding (Table 6.17) which showed Liverpool readers to be less concerned with the Births, Deaths and Marriages column of their local newspapers than were their counterparts in the other cities.

A far clearer picture emerges from Table 6.37 which splits the sample into those who have lived all their lives in the cities and those who have lived for only a part of their lives there. It should come as no surprise that Liverpool is again 'quite contrary'.

Only Liverpool deviates from the predictable pattern, and then only for local radio; apart from Radio Merseyside the finding is consistent across cities and media. Those who have lived all their lives in the locality gain higher average local media gratifications than do those who are relative newcomers, or have lived away from their place of birth for some time. What is more, almost identical distributions are found if the number of years lived in the locality is treated in the same way — the longer the period of residence the higher the average gratification score, except in Liverpool where there is some indication of a reverse tendency. One factor at work here is surely the respondent's embeddedness in the cities' social fabrics. Tables 6.38 and 6.39 turn to this factor in terms of proportion of friends and relatives who live around the respondents.

Table 6.38 is predictable enough, i.e. it shows a more or less consistent tendency for the proportion of relatives living in the locality to be directly related to average communications gratifications. An obvious point should be borne in mind when reading the tables, however, which is that most people find the bulk of their social contacts in the locality. Consequently few of our respondents answered 'Hardly any' to either question and, therefore, some of these percentages are of dubious value. This limitation is frustrating in the case of Table 6.39, since an understandable and interesting result is otherwise suggested. The several-sided social uses of local media are hinted at in this table's pattern.

Some theoreticians have argued that mass media satisfactions are all based upon the role of media as substitutes for, or facilitators of, face-to-face communication. Both these two uses (substitution and facilitation) are indicated by Table 6.39 (if taken at its face value). In several columns we see those with many friends and those with hardly any gaining higher satisfaction than those in the middle with 'a few' friends living around them. Separate processes can therefore be assumed to be working, those with many friends living in the locality using media to help maintain their social relationships, whilst those with hardly any friends around them using the same media as a substitute for social companionship. Returning to the tables, and allowing for possible instability due to small samples, the safest summary would state that, for local radio those who have the majority of their friends and relatives around them gain greater satisfactions from local media than do those who have only a few in

Table 6.37

Average Gratification Scores x Proportion of Life Lived in Locality x Media x City

	Oxford		Hull		Liverpool		Bristol		Nottingham	
	Local Radio	Local Press	Local Radio	Local Press	Local Radio	Local Press	Local Radio	Local Press	Local Radio	Local Press
All of life	6.9	6.8	7.7	9.1	4.5	6.7	4.0	6.8	7.4	6.4
Part of life	5.4	5.8	6.9	7.6	5.3	5.9	3.6	6.2	5.6	6.0

Table 6.38

Average Gratification Scores x Kin in Neighbourhood x Media x City

	Oxford		Hull		Liverpool		Bristol		Nottingham	
	Local Radio	Local Press	Local Radio	Local Press	Local Radio	Local Press	Local Radio	Local Press	Local Radio	Local Press
All/most	7.5	7.3	7.6	9.0	4.8	6.4	4.4	6.6	7.7	6.3
Few	6.5	6.0	7.9	8.3	4.2	7.3	2.9	6.2	4.6	5.5
Hardly any/ none	3.9*	5.0*	4.8*	5.8*	4.2*	6.3*	3.2*	6.5*	4.6*	5.5*

* Based on small proportion of sample

Table 6.39

Average Gratification Scores x Friends in Neighbourhood x Media x City

	Oxford		Hull		Liverpool		Bristol		Nottingham	
	Local Radio	Local Press	Local Radio	Local Press	Local Radio	Local Press	Local Radio	Local Press	Local Radio	Local Press
All/most	6.9	7.2	7.6	8.8	4.9	6.5	4.1	6.9	6.9	6.5
Few	3.4	3.8	6.1	6.8	1.7*	6.3	3.3	6.0	4.7	5.2
Hardly any/ none	7.4*	5.5	7.3*	7.6	5.7	5.7	2.5	4.4	5.5	4.6

*Based on small proportion of sample

Table 6.40

Average Gratification Scores x Household x Media x City

	Oxford		Hull		Liverpool		Bristol		Nottingham	
	Local Radio	Local Press	Local Radio	Local Press	Local Radio	Local Press	Local Radio	Local Press	Local Radio	Local Press
Live alone	5.1	4.0	10.2	9.8	3.4	5.2	5.4	5.9	7.1	7.4
Live with others	6.1	6.5	6.7	8.4	4.8	6.6	3.6	6.6	6.5	6.0

Table 6.41
Average Gratification Scores x Age When Full Time Education Completed x Media x City

	Oxford		Hull		Liverpool		Bristol		Nottingham	
	Local Radio	Local Press	Local Radio	Local Press	Local Radio	Local Press	Local Radio	Local Press	Local Radio	Local Press
15 years or under	7.6	7.5	8.8	8.9	4.9	6.6	4.3	5.9	7.7	6.8
16–18 years	3.5	5.2	4.3	7.0	3.6	6.1	2.6	7.5	3.5	4.6
19 + years	3.5	3.5	2.1	8.6	3.9	6.6	4.0	7.4	3.4	4.3

Table 6.42
Average Gratification Scores x Employment x Media x City

	Oxford		Hull		Liverpool		Bristol		Nottingham	
	Local Radio	Local Press	Local Radio	Local Press	Local Radio	Local Press	Local Radio	Local Press	Local Radio	Local Press
Full time	6.0	6.7	5.5	7.9	5.3	6.6	3.0	6.5	5.5	6.6
Part time	7.0	7.5	7.8	8.3	4.4	6.2	2.8	5.9	6.7	7.0
No job	5.6	4.8	9.0	9.0	4.1	6.5	5.0	6.7	7.5	5.5

Table 6.43

Average Gratification Scores x Membership of Local Committees x Media x City

	Oxford		Hull		Liverpool		Bristol		Nottingham	
	Local Radio	Local Press	Local Radio	Local Press	Local Radio	Local Press	Local Radio	Local Press	Local Radio	Local Press
Member of 1+ committees	7.1	5.8	6.7	8.6	5.4	5.9	4.7	6.3	4.0	5.5
City average	6.0	6.1	7.3	8.4	4.7	6.5	3.8	6.5	6.6	6.2

Table 6.44

Average Gratification Scores x Vote in Last Local Election x Media x City

	Oxford		Hull		Liverpool		Bristol		Nottingham	
	Local Radio	Local Press	Local Radio	Local Press	Local Radio	Local Press	Local Radio	Local Press	Local Radio	Local Press
Voted	6.6	6.8	8.2	8.7	4.7	6.7	4.4	6.7	6.7	7.0
Not voted	5.7	5.8	5.2	7.6	4.7	6.0	2.6	6.5	6.8	5.0

the vicinity. The exceptions are marginal and occur in Hull for local radio and in Nottingham and Liverpool for the local press.

A few more variables concerned with chosen position in the cities' social fabric are considered in further tables. Table 6.40, for example, looks at respondents' households; and how living alone or with others is associated with local communication satisfaction. Here a familiar impression of city distinctions appears again with Hull, Nottingham and Bristol sharing one pattern, Oxford and Liverpool sharing the reverse pattern. Again the two social functions of the media are temptingly apposite — with those living alone apparently seeking substitute companionship, while those who live with others are maximising on the 'coin of exchange' function. Although the substitute companionship hypothesis is quite convincing, since the composition of household largely defines listening context and whilst those who live and listen alone are likely to find some substitute companionship in radio, it does not necessarily follow that they are lonely, or that their main source of companionship is radio. Local press follows a similar general pattern to local radio with the exception of Bristol, where those living in larger households are likely to gain greater satisfaction than respondents who live alone.

Tables 6.41 to 6.44 complete this section of simple background measures and their relationship to average gratification.

It is not our intention to comment on these tables as such but rather to consider what they show, in conjunction with the findings already presented in this section, as part of the broader task of clarifying overall patterns in the associations between respondent background and local media satisfaction. In hunting for such patterns, we ask: which groups, as defined in the tables, are gaining above average gratifications for each city and for each medium? The answer is given below for uses of the press first. Groups are defined by the marginal labels used in the preceding tables.

Table 6.45
Groups Scoring Above Average Gratifications for Local
Evening Paper

Oxford   Male. Working class. 36—55. City/county. Full/part
            job. Voted. All of life. Live with others. Under 15.
            Most friends. Most relatives.

Hull   Female. Middle class. 36+. City. No job. Committee.
            Voted. All of life. Live alone. Under 15/over 19.
            Most friends. Most relatives.

98

Liverpool	Female. Working class. 36—55. City. Full time job. Voted. All of life. Live with others. Under 15/over 19. Most friends. Few kin.
Bristol	Middle class. 36+. City. No job. Voted. All of life. Live with others. 16+. Most friends. Most relatives.
Nottingham	Male. Working class. 36+. City. Full/part job. Voted. All of life. Live alone. Under 15. Most friends. Most/few relatives.

If we extract from Table 6.45 all groups that occur in each list, we can specify those types of people who, regardless of city, appear to gain greatest total satisfaction from reading their local evening paper. The profile reads as follows: Aged between 36 and 55 years, born in the city, lived in the city all of their lives, voted in the last local election and are surrounded by their kith and kin. Interestingly, having extracted that common pattern there is no clear indication of any further patterning; on other variables the cities seem to be quite idiosyncratic although certain pairs of cities do produce some overlaps. The picture is quite different for local radio as can be seen in Table 6.46, which lists those groups that gain above average gratifications from listening to BBC local radio.

Table 6.46
Groups Scoring Above Average Gratifications for Local Radio

Oxford	Working class. 56+. County. Part time job. On committees. Voted. All of life. Live with others. Under 15. All/hardly any friends. All/few relatives.
Hull	Female. Working class. 56+. City/county. Part/no job. Voted. All of life. Live alone. Under 15. All friends. All/few relatives.
Liverpool	Male. Working class. On committee. Part of life. Under 15. 18—55 years. All/hardly any friends. All relatives. City. Full time job.
Bristol	Female. Working class. 36+. City/county. No job. On committees. Voted. All of life. Live alone. Under 15/19+. All friends. All relatives.

Nottingham   Female. Working class. 56+. City/county. Part/no
                job. Not voted. All of life. Live alone. Under 15.
                All friends. All relatives.

Firstly, we can extract those elements that are common to all five
stations, which are: Being working class, born in, or around, the city,
left school at fifteen or younger, and still have the majority of their
friends and relations around them. This, then, is the general picture,
and in many ways it seems to reflect a tight knot of interrelated
factors, which are consistent with each other and perhaps predictable
one from the other. Although there is no *a priori* reason why these
factors should emerge as core variables in explaining high levels of
local media satisfaction, there is reason enough to predict that city
born working class respondents will tend to leave school at fifteen and
have their kith and kin around them.

Unlike the local press results, however, the extraction of common
features has by no means exhausted the patterning of Table 6.46. The
pattern of city comparisons and contrasts suggested previously in the
text, is reinforced rather dramatically. Three cities — Hull, Bristol and
Nottingham — have a further five factors in common, that is, five
specific high-scoring groups common to those three cities, in addition
to the five groups that were common to all five cities. The additional
features shared by Hull, Nottingham and Bristol, are: Female, over
56 years old, no job, or a part time job, lived all of their lives in the
community, and presently living alone. Unlike the list of features
common to all cities, this set cannot be presented as a knot of
interrelated variables. With the possible exception of sex to working
status, there is little predictability from one variable to the other in
the Hull/Bristol/Nottingham list, for sex, age and household are not
related in the same way as, say, social class and level of education
(although it is reasonable to point out that, due to differential
longevity, older women are more likely to be living alone than older
men).

Although the cluster of characteristics shared by three of the cities
is not internally predictable, considered together the variables do seem
to present a recognisable picture of a certain type of person. This is
someone who in previous cultures, and in certain contemporary
cultures other than our own, served a social purpose within a family
unit of which she was still a valued member. Nowadays, however,
such individuals may often suffer from a lack of social contact,
purpose and meaningful activity. It is a comment on our society that
it has tended to isolate certain types of people, who in other times
were (a) less numerous because death occurred, on average at an

100

earlier age, and (b) more socially integrated. The aforementioned 'substitute companionship' use of mass media is clearly relevant here; yet there is also the hint of a more general process whereby certain contemporary media — possibly local ones in particular — can give comfort and meaning to sections of society that are otherwise neglected or deprived. For the members of such groups the notion of 'substitute companionship' may take on a far broader definition and encompass more than a friendly chat. Radio and other sources of local material may provide the sensation of belonging to a community and also serve as interpreters of trends in the 'outside world'. It need not surprise us that it is radio that throws most light on this grouping, for, as evidenced later, radio has a distinctive potential for generating a sense of friendly companionship lacking in newspapers (in this context it is interesting to note the expression 'in cold print').

The preceding paragraph, then, proceeds beyond the readily understandable idea that someone, when alone, can gain satisfaction from hearing a friendly voice, to a more complex conceptualisation which suggests that media can people the social vacuum that sometimes surrounds the elderly. This second version of a social media function entails a far more amorphous process transcending single, particular uses and satisfactions, and featuring a more embracing involvement with a communication source. But the two extremes are caught both in everyday speech and in the philosophies of local broadcasters. For example, informants in group discussions sometimes refer to ' . . . a feeling of belonging in a community', and broadcasters often include in their 'philosophies' the idea of 'community building' — for some, this community is created by media and is electronic rather than social.

Returning to Table 6.46, it is evident that patterns found in Nottingham, Hull and Bristol are not often shared by the two remaining cities, Oxford and Liverpool. However, Oxford is in some respects nearer to the three than it is to Liverpool. For example, it shares with them an emphasis on above average local radio satisfactions among older inhabitants with part time jobs who have lived in the locality all of their lives; but it differs in highlighting those who live with others, rather than alone. Liverpool is quite different from all the other cities. In fact, after extracting the common groups, we are left in its case with something approaching a mirror image of the other stations. Specifically, Liverpool's set of groups scoring high in local satisfactions from radio includes 18 to 55 year old people working full time and individuals who, although born in the city, have lived some part of their lives away from it.[14]

So far we have seen in this section how certain 'background'

101

variables are related to average scores on a scale of total local gratification. Tables 6.45 and 6.46 have shown that both local evening papers and local radio have special appeal to specified 'core groups'. Furthermore, in the case of local radio, we have isolated three cities — Hull, Nottingham and Bristol — that are really rather remarkably similar in terms of the specified groups of their populations that gain greatest satisfaction. Liverpool is the most idiosyncratic city with rather dissimilar groups finding greater satisfaction in the output of its local station from those found in Oxford, and, particularly, those in the remaining three cities.

Do these results shed further light on the question of media complementarity? Although they do not reproduce the impression of a division of functional labour that was fostered by a forced-choice question obliging respondents to choose one medium in preference to another, neither do they suggest that background influences facilitate local communication satisfaction in an identical manner from both local radio and the press. For example, it has already been noted that the press is a source of greater satisfaction for men than women, and that age is differently related to gratifications obtained from the two media. Whilst satisfaction gained from radio increases with age, satisfaction from the local press is spread across our samples with a tendency for the middle aged to secure the highest average gratification. And if we turn to individual cities, there are more examples of complementarity. In both Bristol and Hull, working class respondents gain above average gratification from radio, whilst middle class respondents gain above average gratification from the press; again, in Bristol those who live alone score highly on radio, while those who live with others score highly on the press — a pattern which is reversed for Nottingham. There is some evidence here, then, that, even though the individual gratifications have been summated into an overall score, some groups of city residents are more finely tuned to their local radio stations, while others are more finely tuned to their local newspapers.

One final finding can be extracted from Tables 6.45 and 6.46. We have seen how certain defined groups produced above average scores for local radio in all five cities, and how other groups produced above average scores for the local evening paper of each city, but what of overlap between the media? A further common set of variables can be extracted from the evidence. There is a small number of defined groups which appear on both lists; that is, three background factors are related to above average gratification from both local radio and local evening newspapers. These core groups consist of those who were born in the city and have a majority of friends and relations

102

living around them. It is of some significance that the three features of our samples which relate to both forms of local media consist of two unequivocally social factors, plus the fact of having been born in the city. In as much as local media can be seen as providing services to the 'local community', it is clear that these three groups are probably amongst the best predictors of the feeling of existing within and belonging to a local community. At core, then, we appear to have evidence that local media, both radio and press — at least in part — are satisfying one of the more important general justifications for their existence. They particularly service locally rooted citizens.

The tables presented so far in this section have focused on many variables reflecting the respondents' positions in the fabric of their local communities as well as certain standard demographic measures. Many of these features of our respondents' circumstances will tend to be related, through day to day experience, with their feelings about, or attitudes toward, their city. The reader will recall (p.26) that certain questions from the questionnaire were converted into three scales of civic attitude: importance to the respondent of civic amenities (schools, roads, transport, cinemas and so on), positive feelings about the city (pride, etc.), and a scale of local involvement based upon a combination of the preceding scales.

We are now in a position to consider the relationships between these civic attitudes and average local gratification scores. And again our attention will be directed to questions about the overall patterning of the findings as well as to discrete findings for individual cities as such. Table 6.47 shows the average gratification scores for each medium, in each city, for respondents who were classified High, Medium or Low on the scale of involvement in the city. Common sense suggests that such a scale would relate positively with the attainment of local satisfaction, those who are high on involvement being more likely to find satisfaction in the use of local media than those who feel little involvement in the city.

This is indeed the case. Inspection of the table shows that only in one city does the pattern deviate from our common sense prediction and that is the case of the local press in Nottingham. With this exception the table reveals a satisfyingly consistent picture. Highly involved respondents gain higher average satisfaction than mediumly involved respondents, who, in their turn, gain higher satisfaction than those with low involvement. No evidence here, then, of the three-city pattern which was apparent in the earlier tables; on the other hand, such a pattern is unlikely since the overall relationship between civic involvement and local gratification is so easily predicted.

Clearly the relationship holds for both radio and the press, but

Table 6.47
Local Gratification Scores x Involvement in City

Involvement	Oxford Local Radio	Oxford Local Press	Hull Local Radio	Hull Local Press	Liverpool Local Radio	Liverpool Local Press	Bristol Local Radio	Bristol Local Press	Nottingham Local Radio	Nottingham Local Press
High	9.1	8.9	10.2	9.9	6.1	7.9	5.3	7.3	7.8	7.7
Medium	5.7	5.9	7.1	8.1	4.9	6.7	3.4	6.4	6.5	5.7
Low	4.3	4.8	4.6	7.5	2.5	4.6	2.5	5.6	5.8	6.2

Table 6.47(a)
Differences in Levels of Gratification Between Those Scoring High on Civic Involvement and Those Scoring Low

	Oxford Local Radio	Oxford Local Press	Hull Local Radio	Hull Local Press	Liverpool Local Radio	Liverpool Local Press	Bristol Local Radio	Bristol Local Press	Nottingham Local Radio	Nottingham Local Press
Difference (d)	4.8	4.1	5.6	2.4	3.6	3.3	2.8	1.7	2.0	1.5

Table 6.48

Local Gratification Scores x Importance of Civic Amenities

Importance of Civic Amenities	Oxford		Hull		Liverpool		Bristol		Nottingham	
	Local Radio	Local Press	Local Radio	Local Press	Local Radio	Local Press	Local Radio	Local Press	Local Radio	Local Press
High	8.0	7.4	9.1	9.0	6.0	7.6	4.1	7.4	6.3	6.1
Medium	6.0	6.0	7.2	8.1	4.8	6.3	3.8	6.0	6.2	5.8
Low	4.6	5.6	6.1	8.5	2.6	5.5	3.6	6.7	7.6	7.1
'd'	3.4	1.8	3.0	0.5	3.4	2.1	0.5	0.7	-1.3	-1.0

Table 6.49

Local Gratification Scores x Positive Feelings About the City

Positive Feelings about the city	Oxford		Hull		Liverpool		Bristol		Nottingham	
	Local Radio	Local Press	Local Radio	Local Press	Local Radio	Local Press	Local Radio	Local Press	Local Radio	Local Press
High	8.5	8.2	10.0	11.0	4.6	8.7	4.6	7.0	8.5	7.9
Medium	5.1	5.5	7.0	7.7	5.5	6.7	3.7	6.4	6.6	5.9
Low	5.2	5.3	3.9	6.6	3.0	4.3	2.6	5.7	4.0	4.8
'd'	3.3	2.9	6.1	4.4	1.6	3.4	2.0	1.3	4.5	2.9

there is also some evidence to suggest that degree of involvement is more closely related to gratifications associated with radio than with the press. In effect, the sorting of respondents into high, medium and low scores on involvement has produced a wider range of total gratification for use of one medium than for the other; as we move down the high/medium/low scale, total gratification falls off more sharply for radio than for the press. This effect is clear from inspection of Table 6.47(a), which presents the differences in levels of gratification between high and low categories of involvement on each medium in each city.

The numbers are derived by taking the bottom row of Table 6.47 from the top row. For example, for Oxford, Low = 4.3; High = 9.1; 9.1 - 4.3 = 4.8, which is the difference score entered in Table 6.47(a). In every case 'd' is greater for local radio than it is for the local press. In the next two tables we break Involvement into its two component scales of practical and emotional involvement with 'd' scores shown at the base of each column.

Table 6.47 is based upon a combination of the two scales represented in Tables 6.48 and 6.49; the table is noteworthy for its consistency; the general, summarising scale of 'involvement' in the city is probably the best single predictor of degree of satisfaction found in use of local media. But splitting that scale into its components of practical and emotional civic involvement produces a more complex set of relationships. Whilst in the majority of cases high scorers on the attitude scales are also high scorers in terms of local gratification, there are exceptions. And inspection of the two tables shows that the exceptions contribute to a now familiar pattern, viz., they bring together, Nottingham, Hull and Bristol.

First consider Table 6.48. The attitude scale here measures the importance of specified civic amenities that range from transport systems to educational facilities; earlier the scale was described as one of practical involvement. Obviously local media can feed this type of practical involvement. In the main such a servicing will be reflected in the provision of information — for example, alteration of transport timetables, weather and traffic news, and publicity about 'what's on' in the locality. Predictably enough, then, this scale and the total gratification scale are closely related. But in Bristol practical orientation appears to have little, if any, influence on local gratifications and for Hull and Nottingham satisfaction obtained from the use of local evening papers is related to practical involvement somewhat differently. For local newspapers in these cities the highest amount of satisfaction is found amongst high and low scorers, a relationship which also holds good for Radio Nottingham.

106

Table 6.49 examines the relationship between gratification and emotional involvement in the city and here the predicted relationship between the two scales breaks down for local radio in Liverpool and the local press in Oxford (although, as earlier tables have led us to expect, Oxford falls somewhere between Liverpool and the rest). Summarising this emergent pattern: emotional involvement is most clearly related to local media gratifications in Hull, Nottingham, and Bristol; practical involvement is most clearly related to local media gratifications in Liverpool and Oxford.

Inspection of the differences ('d' scores) between High and Low scores for each table is informative. Practical involvement appears to have little or no influence upon the levels of satisfaction associated with both radio and the press in Bristol and Nottingham, while in the other cities this scale has a greater influence on radio scores than on press scores. Emotional involvement is influential (as indicated by the 'd' scores) to a greater extent for radio than for the press in all cities but Liverpool, where the reverse obtains. But, over-riding these specific variations is the observation that, almost without exception, the emotional scale produces a greater 'd' score for a specified medium and town than does the practical involvement scale. In other words, emotional involvement is, in general, a better predictor of gratifications found in local media than is practical involvement, and, with the exception of Liverpool, emotional involvement in the city is more closely related to level of satisfaction with radio than with the press.

Overall, this last set of tables has reasserted the familiar city groupings, with Liverpool being something of an exception and Oxford located somewhere between Liverpool and the three other cities. Furthermore, although the local press, in general, is the source of greater total gratification than local radio, these scales of civic involvement are rather more closely related to the gratifications derived from local radio listening.

Perhaps the reader should be reminded at this point that the practical-emotional split in civic attitudes was, in the first instance, built into the questionnaire as an imposed rather than emergent distinction. However, this quite meaningful dichotomy has also thrown light upon the distribution of gratifications in our samples, and has further diagnostic use. It could be hypothesised, for example, that the groups of high scorers on our two civic attitude scales might be seeking qualitatively different gratifications. The idea is attractive, but it should be recalled that in the nature of our attitude measurement it is possible to have a high degree of overlap between the two groups of high scorers. A proportion of our sample will be both high on civic pride and high on reliance on civic amenities, and this could cloud the evidence. Nevertheless, it is worth at this stage delving a little more deeply into the structure of local gratifications themselves.

Given thirteen gratification statements, how do they interrelate? Again 'McQuitty's Elementary Linkage Analysis' can be applied. It will be recalled that linkage or 'cluster' analysis correlates all responses which are statistically co-related (see p.28). Such correlated statements can be quite dissimilar; indeed they sometimes appear contradictory.[15] However, the Centre's experience has been pleasantly consistent and repeatedly cluster analysis has produced meaningful clusters of intercorrelated items.

Using a full sample of 1,000 respondents (200 from each city), a cluster analysis of local radio gratification statements produced a four-cluster structure. To the author's delight this emergent structure offered impressive complementary support to the practical-emotional civic involvement distinction.

The first cluster to emerge had a distinctive social, or more correctly, para-social, core to it. The dominant item on which it hinged was: (h) The people on Radio . . . have become like friends to me. Other items in the cluster were: (a) Radio . . . makes me feel like part of a real community, (e) It keeps me in touch with people and places I know, (i) It reminds me what the city was like in earlier days, (j) Radio . . . stands up for things I believe in, and (m) the respondent was capable of naming radio personalities he 'really looks forward to hearing'. In order to be consistent with terminology used by other researchers (particularly Professor Karl-Erik Rosengren of Lund University, Sweden), we will call this cluster Para-social Interaction Gratification, or PSIG. Underlying the theoretical concept of para-social interaction is the thought that audience members react to broadcasters as if the broadcaster was addressing them personally. A corollary is that consciously, or non-consciously, certain broadcasters adopt a style of presentation that encourages this feeling of contact.

In fact, the phrase 'para-social interaction' was originally coined by D. Horton and R. Wohl (1956) to describe the kind of relationship which might exist between the presenter of a television 'chat' show and his or her audience. Presenters of such shows, Horton and Wohl noted, behaved towards their audiences as if in face-to-face contact, i.e. they employed a number of techniques to create an impression of long term familiarity and friendship with audience members. For example, the presenter was likely to make frequent references to close relatives and friends as if the audience were acquainted with them.

('Gee, my wife, Mary, would truly love that.') Such a presenter never failed to exploit unexpected noise in the studio in order to let the audience member in on the act. ('Ooops. There goes Fred again. Fred's our studio manager, folks. Keep on dropping things and we'll put glue on your fingers Fred.') The style is familiar to Radio One listeners and local radio has its own variant: 'Here comes Pat with what looks like a correction to that last announcement'.

Just as the broadcasting techniques which encourage 'para-social interaction' have spread, so too the concept itself has been found useful in the interpretation of findings from a number of uses and gratification studies. It is no longer limited to the television chat show audience but can be applied to all those listening and viewing occasions when the audience member is asked at one and the same time to maintain his or her identity and to interact with the broadcaster. The items in cluster I relate quite clearly to this concept: . . . become like friends to me . . . part of a real community . . . people and places I know . . . stands up for things I really believe in . . . and, the ability to name favourite radio personalities.

After extracting PSIG Cluster I, seven items remained, which interrelated as follows:

Cluster II: (e) Gives an interesting local slant on national news stories (dominant item).
(f) Tells me what ordinary people are thinking and talking about.
(k) It tells me about new developments in the city.

Cluster III: (b) . . . good way for me to find out what is going on in and around the city.
(c) I sometimes talk about things I've heard on Radio . . .

Cluster IV: (d) I find the local weather and road reports useful.
(g) Radio . . . keeps me well informed about local sports.

These secondary clusters have affinities with each other in as much as all contributory items are concerned with the provision of information. It would appear that by following the procedures outlined (extensive qualitative work and piloting) we have produced findings that suggest a major two part structure of local communications gratifications, i.e. a split into PSIG (para-social interaction) and information-based gratification. At this point the investigator, who

109

speaks no Greek, will probably be forgiven for emitting the cry, 'Bingo'. Here is a remarkably obvious parallel between the components of civic attitude and the components of local communications gratifications associated with local radio listening. And this is no mere statistical conjury but a genuinely emergent relationship that was not deliberately built into the research, nor even foreseen.

Civic attitude, on the basis of group discussions, was broken into two components: practical involvement and emotional involvement. Local radio gratifications, themselves derived from group discussions, were found to have a two part statistical structure: para-social interaction gratification, and information-based gratification. It has already been argued that practical involvement, as measured by the salience of several civic amenities, calls for a ready stream of information about the locality which ranges from the 'narrowly utilitarian' road and weather reports through to general debate on, for example, local education facilities and redevelopment. It is equally apparent that emotional involvement will be fed by para-social interaction with its underlying basis in the 'friendly local' station that reminds us of the city's early days and stands up for things we believe in. Our penultimate dip into the data has thrown up a seemingly neat and tidy theoretical package.

The two dichotomies are related in terms of their apparent meaning; that is beyond dispute. But is there also an empirical relationship? Furthermore, is the three city pattern still in evidence at this level of empirical analysis? To answer these questions we must present Table 6.50, which shows average scores on the two gratification components, PSIG and information, for high, medium, and low scorers on measures of civic attitude.[16]

The most marked feature of this table is its consistency; in every condition information-based satisfaction exceeds PSIG. It will be remembered that the two scales have been standardised; therefore this finding is unlikely to be related to the fact that the original inventory contained more information items than PSIG items. On the basis of this study, then, we must conclude that local radio, as represented by the five BBC stations under investigation, is more often adapted to the provision of information-based satisfactions than to para-social interaction gratifications.

Another possibility in considering this finding, and one of considerable practical importance to the uses and gratifications approach to mass media studies, is that we have now reached one of the boundaries of this form of empirical research. This question is taken up in the discussion section of this report, for the present it is

Table 6.50
Average Scores on Two Components of Local Gratification
x Civic Involvement

Oxford	Practical Involvement				Emotional Involvement			
	High	Medium	Low	d	High	Medium	Low	d
PSIG	5.8	3.6	2.8	(3.0)	5.8	3.0	3.6	(2.2)
Information	7.3	5.8	4.7	(2.6)	7.0	5.1	4.9	(2.1)
Hull								
PSIG	6.0	4.2	3.8	(2.2)	6.8	4.2	1.8	(5.0)
Information	8.6	7.3	6.0	(2.6)	9.0	7.0	4.4	(4.6)
Liverpool								
PSIG	4.0	2.8	1.6	(2.4)	3.0	3.4	1.6	(1.4)
Information	5.8	4.9	2.6	(3.2)	4.4	5.4	3.1	(1.3)
Bristol								
PSIG	3.2	2.6	2.4	(0.8)	3.6	2.6	1.0	(2.6)
Information	3.6	3.6	3.4	(0.2)	4.0	3.4	3.0	(1.0)
Nottingham								
PSIG	4.0	3.6	5.2	(-1.2)	5.6	4.0	2.0	(3.6)
Information	6.1	6.3	7.1	(-1.0)	8.1	6.3	4.1	(4.0)

sufficient to note that the approach employed in this study can only directly measure the more conscious and apparent uses of media. It is likely that the motives that link people to media range from manifest, conscious, deliberate uses (road and weather reports, time checks, and so on) through to the darker hinterlands of our non-conscious processes which fuel the work of psycho-analysts and other 'depth' theoreticians. Perhaps para-social interaction with media figures represents a borderline case which our 'string and wire' technology underestimates and distorts. Certainly audience members can be expected to vary in their degree of insight into the types of relationships that exist between them and broadcast material; research of the type recorded here is, in a non-derogatory sense, then, superficial and aimed at mapping the surface rather than plumbing the depths. But of course, the two types of satisfaction, information-based gratification and PSIG, are not mutually exclusive; maybe optimal local broadcasts provide the basis for a balance of both gratifications.

Within the consistent result of information-gratification domination, the familiar three-city pattern emerges once again. Consider, for example, the highest scorers for each city: in Oxford and Liverpool greatest satisfaction is found amongst those who are classified High on practical orientation to the city; for the remaining three cities it is those who score High on emotional orientation to the city. This reinforces the earlier speculations generated by isolating those defined groups who recorded above average gratification scores in the three cities and were crudely labelled 'deprived'. Members of such groups would surely be characterised by an emotional orientation to both their city and their local media. The pattern also emerges if we consider the 'd' or difference columns in Table 6.50. By taking Low scores from High scores we arrive at 'd'. The greater is the relationship between civic attitude and gratification the larger is 'd', this because the measure of civic attitude has succeeded in splitting respondents into those gaining more or less satisfaction (PSIG or information). Inspection of 'd' columns, noting the highest values for each city, reveals the following:

> Oxford *practical* orientation most closely related to *PSIG.*
> Liverpool *practical* orientation most closely related to
>   *information.*
> Hull *emotional* orientation most closely related to *PSIG.*
> Bristol *emotional* orientation most closely related to *PSIG.*
> Nottingham *emotional* orientation most closely related to
>   *information.*

How has the postulated relationship between pairs of civic attitude and local gratification components fared in this empirical testing? In three cities the predicted result occurs: practical/information, or emotional/PSIG. Not too bad then. But, if we consider the two cities where the hypothesis is not borne out, Oxford and Nottingham, we find the second highest relationship for each city is in line with the hypothesis: Oxford, information/practical, and Nottingham, PSIG/

emotional. After a long journey we should not be dissatisfied when we score three bulls and two inners. And we can terminate the presentation of results on the happy note of the revealed three city consistency. These clear patterns raise questions enough and they will influence the shape and content of the next chapter. Our main objective is to overview the study's findings by returning to certain theoretical speculations and themes. The pattern to look for now is conceptual rather than empirical.

NOTES

[1] An important point when comparing the results of this survey with those produced by, for example, the BBC Audience Research Department since BBC 'patronage' figures include children of five years and over. These are also city samples, not comparable with the routine measurements by BBC ARD or JICRAR.
[2] I am aware the Dirty Old Town refers to Salford — it's just that the Liverpudlian sings it with more feeling.
[3] Responses to items were inter-correlated and then clustered using McQuitty's Elementary Linkage Analysis. These techniques are designed to show how far items are statistically related. Clusters of items (i.e., highly correlated items) feature one 'dominant' item which has the highest average correlation with all other members of the cluster.
[4] Overall rank position is calculated by summating the numerical value of each rank position, e.g., Hull = 3+3+3+3+4, Oxford = 5+5+4+3+2. The smaller the 'sum of ranks', the higher the position in overall ranking.
[5] Careful scrutiny of large scale maps reveals that a straight line could be drawn which would join Liverpool and Bristol!
[6] Of course it can be argued that insidious bias is the most dangerous and that asking direct questions cannot hope to reveal insidious bias.
[7] See Ray Brown, 'Children's Uses of Media', in Brown (ed.) *Children and Television,* Collier Macmillan, London, 1976.
[8] What cannot be stated is whether the changing pattern of sought gratification reflects more than a changing audience — that must await a more detailed investigation.
[9] By way of comparison, the top fives for Radio One, with its rather limited range of content, are encompassed by nine items. Taking just those items that appear in the lists of at least four cities reveals a rather less well balanced set: good company, keeps me

113

cheerful, time checks, relaxing, pass the time. The emphasis is on mood management plus the narrowly utilitarian 'time check' item.

[10] A few years ago I met some children in Scotland who had only ever seen one film, but that one film remained as an influence on their orientation to media − it was a police sponsored film on road safety in the village school.

[11] See R. Brown, J.K. Cramond and R.J. Wilde, 'Displacement Effects of Television and the Child's Functional Orientation to Media'. in Blumler and Katz (eds), *The Uses of Mass Communications,* Sage Publications, Beverly Hills.

[12] For example, Rosengren and Windhahl, 1972.

[13] Since scales were based on twelve items, ' . . . makes me feel like part of a real community', and so on, (excluding item 'm' on the grounds already explained, p.44) the mean has a theoretical range of zero (0 x 12) to 24(2 x 12). Because proportions of our samples did not expose themselves to a particular medium, and thus were not questioned but automatically scored zero, however, actual range is narrower than the theoretical range.

[14] Before leaving these thumbnail sketches of the respondents who are gaining greatest overall satisfaction from local media a word of caution is called for, the combined groups, for example − women, 56+ living alone, are not necessarily the highest scorers, in the general population, but it is in this category that we would expect to find a majority of people who find local radio satisfactory.

[15] For example, consider racial prejudice: agreement with the statement, ' . . . pay any kind of money to get into a good area', will often correlate highly with, ' . . . are unwilling to be integrated, they just have a ghetto mentality'.

[16] The two components of gratification are formed, here, by unequal numbers of items. In order to allow comparison between scores on the information cluster of items and scores on the PSIG cluster of items the data have been standardised so that both clusters are scored on a scale that runs from zero to 10, this is a simple arithmetic procedure comparable with re-expressing 'raw' figures as percentages.

7 Discussion

The Walking Research Report Blues [1]

. . . be nice,
Says the stranger, with his plastic cup,
If in the last few pages you can tie it all up,
Neat and tidy, like in the story books.
I just smile an' give him one of those looks.

I guess this guy believes in Father Christmas.

This report has been selective. And the research it describes was also selective. Just as it would be impossible to conduct an exhaustive investigation of all facets of audience attitudes to local media, so too would it be difficult (an understatement) to report in entirety every scrap of data collected by this piece of research. Researchers are necessarily selective; our selectivity is guided by theory and experience, intuition and expediency. Of course if we are over selective and allow theory to have an undue influence upon our fieldwork, analysis and write-up, then we can sometimes 'tie it all up'. But the lay person is likely to smell a rat; story books are story books, and research reports are research reports. Not that the author wishes to prove his integrity by offering only a handful of sore thumbs . . .

We have taken a particular path through the data, a path paved with fifty empirical tables, and we have manipulated the data in certain ways. Others would have taken different routes, used different techniques. In this chapter we should consider some of the more consistent findings, findings that might be expected to have appeared on almost any track through the data. And we shall also look back to certain ideas that have been introduced to cope with inconsistencies evident in, and questions raised by, the preceding sections. Our present aim, then, is not to review Tables 6.1 to 6.50, nor to impose fixed and firm interpretations and explanations — if so inclined, readers may do that for themselves. Our purpose is rather to clarify some critical issues of interpretation and to present informed speculation about them.

The uses and gratifications approach is one that emphasises individual activity, manipulation and adaptability. It replaces the question, 'What does the medium do to the people?', with, 'What do people do with the medium?'. The idea of an audience made up of identical, passive units is alien to uses and gratifications research, and this suggests that the approach is particularly relevant to the study of local media.

Few who work on the local press or in local radio disagree with the approach's basic assumptions; they know all too well that their audience has a flesh and blood reality, is formed by distinct individuals and is anything but passive. Whilst the local journalist will, perhaps, entertain some abstract image of his or her audience, he or she will also repeatedly meet members of this audience — in the pub, back garden and street. Of course stars of the national media also meet members of their audiences, but there is a distinct difference. In a very real sense the local audience is clustered around the local medium and its personnel; it is formed by individuals who share a hundred and one points of contact and interaction. Compared with this, the national audience — be it ever so large — is a frail ghost, an abstract conception, a creature of far flung cells part realised only at the occasional free pop concert. Moreover the local media are a part of the locality, or community; the relationship is more organic and intimate and less determined by rules of law, custom and scheduling than that shared by national media with the national audience.

On the other hand, the local press shares many of its strengths and weaknesses with the national press, and the same applies to local and national radio. The relationship with its audience may be organic, but it is also shaped by characteristics of media which are unrelated to the locality. Furthermore, in the case of newspapers and radio those characteristics are different, and consequently the experience of exposure to them is also different.

A simple distinction can be made between the properties, or characteristics, of a medium, and the content (programmes, articles, etc.) of that medium. In this report we have set local radio in the context of radio as such (same medium, different content) and in the context of local communications (different media, greater correspondence of content). It was not a task of our project to compare national radio programmes with local radio programmes, but a comparison of some of the properties of local radio and local press is pertinent.

Once turned on and tuned in, we can listen to radio without using anything but our ears, no need to turn over pages, straighten them out, find a flat surface, or a comfortable chair. Whereas reading a newspaper is usually a private activity, one that is different to share until after the event, radio allows a number of people to listen at the same time in the same room. These commonplace observations are rather important when we consider the uses and gratifications associated with radio and the press.[2]

A medium which allows us satisfaction whilst we go about our business can be a blessing. Drivers can listen to radio when driving to or from work, in factories we can listen without being distracted from the task at hand, and the sting is taken from many other activities by listening to radio — washing up, interior decorating, and so on. When asked, for each section of the day, whether they were 'just listening' or 'doing something else as well', listeners produced the following answers (averaged across the five cities): 78 per cent listened whilst doing something else before nine o'clock, between nine and one o'clock 76 per cent listened whilst doing something else, in the afternoon the figure was 74 per cent, and in the evening, 53 per cent of those listening to radio were doing something else at the same time. Clearly, newspapers do not offer the same freedom in the selection of suitable accompanying activities, which can be counted on the fingers of one hand: whilst being driven to work, whilst eating, whilst bathing and . . . the writer has no intention of going any further.

Although both media have delayed social uses, i.e. in providing topics of conversation, radio includes two other social elements in its repertoire of uses. First, as has already been observed, two or more persons can listen at the same time, passing comments, laughing together, speculating on the outcomes of plays or the implications of a news item. Averaging across the four periods of the listening day and across all cities, questions five to nine showed that, of those who listened at some period in the day preceding questioning, 55 per cent did so in the company of someone else.[3] A second social element is provided by the very voices that issue from our radio receivers; radio can provide 'company' but print cannot. And, since we seem to be listing some of the strengths of radio not shared by the press, radio can provide music, bird song and drama whilst the press can only describe, analyse or comment on them.

But the newspaper also has its strengths and perhaps the greatest is the degree of control given to the reader over its uses. We can fully determine the sequence in which we read our paper, and the time taken over particular items. We can read and re-read, clip sequences out and send them to distant friends. We can carry the paper with us to a public meeting and quote from it. We can say, 'Look at this', followed, after a suitable pause, by, 'What do you think of that?'. If radio is a set meal (though, for many, local radio provides no menu: Table 6.21), the newspaper is a smorgasbord.

The content of these two local media is often quite similar, since it is shaped by the same local events and developments, but, as already mentioned, some types of content are allowed to one medium and denied the other: whilst radio exploits sound, the press exploits vision, 'spot the ball' and 'crosswords' vs. 'musical interludes', pictures of Old Coventry vs. the sound of a bombing raid. And not only do the physical properties of a medium impose constraints upon its content; so too does the method of financing. BBC local radio cannot accept paid advertising, but with its dedications, requests and 'swop shops' it presents an informal personal column. (Death, on local radio, is limited to the accident prone, the murder victim and the famous, but we can all get our deaths announced in the local paper. [4]) The local paper, on the other hand, relies on advertising revenue, and, as we have seen, many people make a point of reading the advertisements in their local papers. Just as BBC radio cannot accept advertising revenue, local radio must also avoid campaigning in local or national politics, since the BBC Charter calls for impartiality and balance. Of course, this is an ideal rather than a fully achieved reality, since the very language we use necessarily carries its own partial overtones, but BBC local radio stations are required to aim for this ideal. Local newspapers are not saddled with this constraint, although, in some instances, editorial policy may dictate it. Therefore, the local press can take an overtly 'party political' stance; at most radio assumes a non-conscious or covert 'political' stance.

One of the key issues posed by our gratifications evidence concerns the picture it conveys of inter-relations between the two major parts of the communications environments of our cities, the local radio stations and the local evening papers. Should we see them as sharing a functional division of labour, one medium catering for certain needs while the other serves others? Or should they be thought of as largely addressing the same needs? In the latter event, is it as if they are in competition to demonstrate to would-be audience members that they can meet those needs more satisfactorily than their rival can? On these matters the data seem to point in several directions at once. Although, for example, there were many signs of gratification overlap between the two media, there were also three strands of evidence that were consistent with a complementary relationship.

In a forced-choice question, we saw evidence for a sharing out of gratifications, some best served by radio, some by the press. When looking at those groups of citizens who gained above average gratification in local communication terms, we noted that whilst some were particularly dependent on the press, others turned more often to radio. And finally, in the preceding lines we have mentioned some of the distinctive differences between the two media that were not necessarily tapped by this research.

On these grounds alone, it seems unlikely that the two media are involved in an overall across-the-board competition; neither one could ever fully displace the other. On the other hand, the introduction of local radio has doubtless had some effect on readers' orientations to the local press, just as a change in the press would influence listeners' orientations to local radio — the listener and the reader are often consubstantial. And whilst one listener, having heard the local news, may decide not to read the local paper, another will be moved to seek out the paper in order to follow up some specific news item. Furthermore, these two media need not be competing for the citizens' time since we have already seen that the majority of listeners treat listening as an accompanied activity, i.e. they listen during time which couldn't be given over to reading.

To assume conflict or competition is to neglect the equally applicable interpretation which suggests that local media are symbiotic. And the possibility that the two local media are symbiotic, or mutually beneficial, should not be overlooked since it suggests more than complementarity in the sense of 'carving up the market'. The symbiotic relationship would involve a complex interaction in which exposure to one medium would enhance the use of the other medium. This point was made in the discussion of the ways in which radio and press may interact in their coverage of 'events' present, past and future. There it was argued that having been informed of a local event by local radio the listener might then attend the event and thus be more inclined to read about it in the local press. Many other examples can be given, the broadcast debate on new catchment areas for our local schools draws our attention to an informative map presented in the local press, or, after hearing an account of the local 'derby' match, we turn to the evening paper to relive the game and read informed opinion on its consequences. And both media often advertise each other's content, the local evening paper by printing the day's programmes, and the radio station often broadcasting a 'What the local papers say' item. In a more general sense the stimulation or regeneration of interest in the locality by one medium is likely to result in an increased awareness of other local media.[5]

This symbiotic thesis is consistent with a view of the wider local communications environment as a complex, overlaid and interwoven matrix that includes parish magazines, notice boards, street hand-outs and so on. If we accept that contact with others and conversation is also an element of the local communications environment, then we find another indication of the rich inter-connection of media, for now one of the prevalent gratifications of media, 'Gives me something to talk about', the so-called 'coin of exchange' function, itself becomes an input to the communications environment. At its very simplest this idea is seen in the tendency for friends and colleagues to direct us to certain programme repeats or to save an issue of the local paper for us. And often, the direction is accompanied by comments on the programmes, stated expectations or a request — implicit or explicit — that we should get together and talk about it later.

The point is that whereas it is tempting for empirical research to be conducted 'as if' the communications environment was a static, firmly structured and externally objectifiable entity, a little thought and introspection highlights a different reality. Of course, we can list elements in the environment — radio, press, canteen chat, etc., but that tells us little about the experiential reality of our communications environment. What does it feel like? If the reader will now, as it were, experience his or her location in the communications environment, we might reach an agreement that 'complexity' is almost inadequate as a descriptive label. We are rather dealing with a busy, fluid, disjointed 'system': bits and pieces of the mass media, half-remembered documentaries, unfinished novels, a crumpled Sunday newspaper beside the bed, Warhol's Marilyn on the lavatory door, Granny upstairs singing Marie Lloyd and our off-spring downstairs listening to Pink Floyd. And that, of course, is not all; the experienced reality of the communications environment transcends time and space — memory and association ensure that. And, in yet another sense, media allow us to transcend time and space, for they not only take us back to our childhood and earlier, they also transport us to meetings we cannot attend and to countries we cannot visit; they are extensions of our senses and . . . they make us feel like part of a 'real' community.

Where does such a flight of fancy fit in with our present research with its fifty tables and defined sample quotas? Underneath it. The research approach adopted here operates on the communications environment at a level which is somewhere between the objective study of local media, their distribution, organisation and financial structure and the purely subjective experience of the communications environment. The strength of this level of operation lies in its presentation of general statements about the audience: 26 per cent of the Oxford sample agreed that Radio Oxford produces a sense of 'real' community, and 40 per cent felt this way about the local evening paper. But what did the eighty individuals who agreed with this statement about the local press actually mean? Another level of entry would be necessary if we were to try to answer that question. It would involve the researcher in more extensive contact with the individual *qua* individual. Such an approach might even elicit a different pattern of results. As suggested earlier, for example, a more intensive study of individuals might move the emphasis on information-based gratifications (for local radio) to the more personal para-social gratifications. And individual, or ideographic, studies would certainly throw up highly idiosyncratic uses and gratifications not covered in our questionnaires. This much is evidenced by group discussions which, themselves, were located somewhere between the levels of our empirical survey work and the truly ideographic study.

If, then, we cannot exactly specify what each respondent had in mind when he or she agreed with a particular item, we can identify certain alternative interpretations. Important distinctions here concern whether the statement is interpreted as relating to 'real' experience or to 'as if' experience, whether the satisfaction is derived from the maintenance of social contacts, or the substitution/replacement/displacement of real contact by mediated contact, or by the sensation of real contact. Bearing these distinctions in mind, we can appreciate that, within the patterns of reported results, quite different systems may be operating. For some individuals, the local press and local radio maintain or even increase their actual involvement in the community; each local gratification featured in this study is consistent with that process. And few would deny the commendability of local media contributions to such an integrative process. Substitution is a different matter, however, for it can be argued that by providing the sensation of community, or companionship without the reality of face-to-face contact, modern media, including local media, are dysfunctional, that they wean some of us away from social contact and thus, over time, dissolve the community network. But for some that community network no longer represents an effective force. The old, the sick, the alienated — in such groups we can locate individuals who have little hope of immediate or even longer term social integration— and for them local media may be the only available source of 'community satisfaction'. Community satisfaction? A sense of social purpose, of belonging — we are led to believe that there used to be a lot more of it around and that it is good for us. Here is Vonnegut, standing psychopharmocology on its head: ' . . . we are full of chemicals which require us to belong to folk societies, or failing that, to feel lousy all the time'(1971).

It is surely no accident that the core groups of high scorers in terms of local gratifications are defined in terms which emphasise community ties, past or present. For both the local press and local radio, and in all five cities, the same three groups of people were gaining above average gratification: those born in the city, those with friends living around them, those with relations living in the vicinity. This finding tends to suggest a creditable general social function for local media of tending to maintain communities, since, as suggested earlier, these characteristics are amongst the best predicters of the feeling of existing in a community. Considering just those groups scoring above average gratification from local radio (Table 6.46) adds to the previous three groups, which were common to radio and the press, a further two: working class, and finished full time education at fifteen years, or younger. But, as will be recalled, Table 6.46 also featured the tendency for three cities, Hull, Bristol and Nottingham, to produce similar results. In this case the cities had in common a further five groups scoring above average gratification. Putting together the group descriptions defines a section of the public containing many who are more likely than most to, in Vonnegut's choice phrase, 'feel lousy all the time': older women, with no job (and, therefore, reduced opportunity for social contact), who have lived all their lives in the community but now live alone.[6] Here then is an indication of substitute companionship and probably an example of local radio playing a broader role than the simple one of bringing voices into the home. But we can go no further; the results cannot reveal whether for these individuals local radio is usefully satisfying those who are beyond integration with the community (for personal reasons, or because no community actually exists), or whether local radio in these three cities is itself helping to isolate certain individuals by encouraging the substitution of media-based satisfactions for 'the real thing' (though on the face of it the first of these hypotheses seems more plausible). And, of course, there is a third possibility: along with substitute companionship, these people may be maximising satisfaction by exploiting local radio in an attempt to maintain real existing contacts, or indeed to initiate new contacts. But why the similarities of Hull, Nottingham and Bristol, and why was Liverpool so consistently contrary?

In the last few paragraphs we have seen how quite different processes could have severally promoted the local gratification results, and we have also seen that in one of these hypothesised processes, local radio was even seen as acting against the spirit of local community.[7] It is possible that the three city pattern is the outcome of local radio stations being shaped by their audience, or vice versa. Certainly our findings indicate considerable differences between some cities, and marked similarities between others. What are the implications of this pattern for those cities not included in our sample? Where would they fall? How many would share Liverpool's idiosyncracies? Our sampling of cities is in no sense representative of the country as a whole, and there is no single measure contained in this study which gives a definitive answer to why the cities emerged as they did. But we can speculate.

Liverpool is the largest city studied, but size alone cannot explain the pattern. If that were the case, then Bristol would follow close on Liverpool, rather than Oxford which is the smallest city. But Liverpool is also characterised in our tables by indications of tightly-knit community, or communities, and in popular imagery this is also the case. And if the maintenance of a pronounced city accent is indicative of social integration, then, out of the five cities Liverpool must be the winner. A crude argument, but one which allows the prediction that Glasgow and Birmingham would be more likely to follow Liverpool than would, say, Manchester or Leeds.

At least the 'strong community' argument is consistent with the 'community satisfactions' assumption discussed above, if Liverpool already has community satisfaction in abundance, then its citizens will tend to exploit both their built and communications environments in a special way. Liverpool respondents, it will be recalled, produced the overall highest score on the practical component of civic attitude, but the lowest on emotional involvement. Perhaps their type of emotional involvement evades the net of our rather straightforward, possibly even banal, scale. (Liverpool's Catholic Cathedral, surely one of the most beautiful of our contemporary buildings, becomes for the self-deflating, satirical Liverpudlian, 'Paddy's Wigwam', or, 'The Mersey Funnel', and the tale of the winking Liver Bird is told against the city's sisters and daughters.)

But since hypothetical explanations of the patterning of our five cities cannot, for the moment, be tested, it is best that we simply consider some of the factors that may have been influential. Perhaps the cities vary in terms of 'ethos', perhaps the local media themselves produce the pattern, perhaps the differences are due to more concrete dissimilarities in the five communications environments. (Note, for instance, that the two exceptions, Oxford and Liverpool, have in common a significant local weekly paper, which is not the case for the three remaining cities.) In the absence of one simple explanation, it is best to assume the realistic position that the pattern reflects a complex interaction of several elements and dimensions with, perhaps, an emphasis on the importance of community satisfaction and the substitute or compensatory role that may be played by local media.

One final sequence of speculation relates to this last point and brings up the issue of para-social interaction. For each city we can calculate the average PSIG score, that is the extent to which individual citizens gain satisfactions related to companionship, the friendliness of local radio, a feeling that local radio stands up for them and so on. The averages are as follows: Oxford 1.9, Hull 2.3, Liverpool 1.4, Bristol 1.4, and Nottingham 2.1. Here is some indication that Liverpool scores lower on these para-social gratifications, but then so, too, does Bristol. The pattern is regained if, instead of thinking in terms of contribution to the city, we consider just those who choose to use local radio. The city pattern of average PSIG scores for listeners is quite different: Bristol 4.2, Hull 3.4, Nottingham and Oxford equal with 3.1, and Liverpool 2.7. It seems, then, that those who use local radio in Liverpool are less likely to achieve PSIG — and again, this is consistent with the assumption that para-social interaction, or this 'local' variant at least, is of less value to those who are embedded in a vital community.

If this is so, and if Liverpool does indeed represent a more adequate grouping of communities or 'folk societies' than the other cities, we are left with certain cliff-hangers concerning particularly Hull, Bristol and Nottingham. Is there a possibility that, for some inhabitants at least, local radio in these cities is proving dysfunctional? We are in no position to say.[8] The alternatives are there, for different groups high PSIG scores may be an indication of valuable community maintenance, valuable solace to those who are unable to experience community as such, or a speeding up of the process often blamed on the mass media — community breakdown.

One further point on this front, however, is that almost all local media do make some direct attempt to involve people in the community or, as it were, to bring the community to some of those who are excluded. Local welfare and charitable organisations, for example, are given free publicity, and in winter time we are reminded to bear in mind the plight of the sick, aged and bedridden. Perhaps advertising free sheets should be excluded from this 'roll of honour', although some may play a part. On the other hand, community news sheets, those often badly reproduced A4 newspapers that are increasingly in evidence, deserve particular credit for their attempts to mobilise and revitalise communities in most practical ways.

With hindsight the split of local gratifications associated with radio into two components, PSIG and information gratifications, need not surprise us. Local radio tries hard to please, its presenters modify their regional accent until they are producing the right Radio X sound, friendliness is emphasised at all times.

Arthur Miller defined a good newspaper as a Nation talking to itself, and this definition is very well suited to local media, particularly local radio. Nation, Speaking Peace Unto Nation, is silenced by the 'democratised microphone' which allows our neighbour to broadcast his grandmother's recipe for mint toffees. The phone-in, a regular feature of most local radio stations, allows a degree of access to this medium which is denied by every form of communication bar conversation and some public meetings. And phone-ins really do allow the community to hear itself, they also allow the local station the opportunity to become more responsive to its audience's needs and interests. From the perspective of para-social interaction the phone-in can become a realisation of an otherwise phantisised, or imagined, interaction. And, for those who simply listen to this type of programme, it offers opportunities for identification or para-social interaction with a wide range of 'ordinary' people. This last point introduces rather more complexity into the notion of PSIG and its consequences for the community. It would seem that the fully democratised microphone becomes the property of a community rather than a service offered to those who live in a locality.

The preceding sentence would be a suitable end to this report, it is soothing and suggestive of local media as full of glorious, soon to be realised, promise, but by tradition research reports are baroque begging letters which end by emphasising that further research is essential and how little we know. The writer has decided to flout convention by not drawing attention to the fact that local communications is an extremely important area of study which requires far more research attention than it presently receives.

NOTES

[1] Quoted, with the author's permission, from, *After Dylan: We're All Tambourine Men Now*, Danny Goldman, unpublished ms.
[2] Of course everybody knows that two or more people can hear the same programme in the same room. Unfortunately, it is these very simple points that social scientists tend to ignore. I make no excuse for stating the obvious.
[3] Percentages reporting accompanied listening for each period of the day: 55 per cent before 9 am, 50 per cent between 9 am and 1 pm, 57 per cent between 1 pm and 6 pm, and 58 per cent after 6 pm.
[4] In fact Manx Radio, the national station of the Isle of Man, does run a regular 'deaths column', but, as with local press, it is only the newsworthy who get a free announcement.
[5] It is worth noting that any of the three types of relationship —

conflict, complementarity, and symbiosis — can be assumed to exist by media personnel themselves, furthermore, the assumption might tend to influence content and, on occasions, become self justifying.

[6] There is a marked similarity between these social groups and those identified in an earlier study conducted by the writer and colleagues Jay G. Blumler and Denis McQuail. In that investigation female fans of *The Dales* were interviewed, the programme was shown to have several distinct types of gratification and amongst those who gained above average gratification were: the middle aged and elderly, those who had been born into large families, those who were living in small households at the time of interview. Of particular importance to Dales fans was the programme's provision of companionship. 'What our evidence about this programme suggested, however, was that the companionship element was even stronger than is often supposed: the characters may become virtually real, knowable and cherished individuals, and their voices are more than just a comforting background that breaks the silence of an empty house'. Denis McQuail, Jay G. Blumler and J.R. Brown, (1972), 'The television audience: a revised perspective', in McQuail, D. (ed.), *Sociology of Mass Communications,* Penguin Books.

[7] The local press is a less likely candidate for this social dysfunction. Since it lacks the 'warm friendly human quality' of radio, it seems unlikely that many would actually prefer it to the 'warm friendly human quality' of a healthy community.

[8] This analysis of para-social interaction gratification argues that the consequences of para-social interaction may be either positive or negative in as much as the listener may use radio content to help maintain real social contact, or to replace real social contact. There is a parallel here with the idea of escapist uses of the mass media. Escapism is often assumed to be, at best, worthless time wasting, positively dangerous, but a little introspection suggests that the consequences of escapist activity may be positive or negative. For example, escapism may allow us to neglect problems to our detriment or it may allow us to distance ourselves from problems and then approach them with renewed vigour and insight. See: Katz, E. and Foulkes, D. (1962), 'On the uses of mass media "escape": clarification of a concept', *Public Opinion Quarterly,* vol.126, pp.372 —88, and Ray Brown (1976), 'Children's uses of television', in Brown (ed.), *Children and Television.*

Bibliography

Blumler, J.G. and Katz, E. (eds), *The Uses of Mass Communications,* Sage Publications Inc., USA, 1974.

Brown, R., Cramond, J.K. and Wilde, R.J., 'Displacement effects of television and the child's functional orientation to media', in Blumler and Katz (eds), *The Uses of Mass Communications,* Sage Publications Inc., USA, 1974.

Brown, R., 'Children's uses of media', in Brown, R. (ed.), *Children and Television,* Collier Macmillan, London; Sage Publications Inc., USA, 1976.

Horton, D. and Wohl, R., 'Mass communication and para-social interaction', *Psychiatry,* vol.XIX, pp.215–29, 1956.

Jones, D., *Talking with People: An Account of the North Devon Project,* forthcoming.

Katz, E. and Foulkes, D., 'On the use of mass media as escape: clarification of a concept', *Public Opinion Quarterly,* vol.LXII, 1962.

McQuail, D., Blumler, J., and Brown, R., 'The television audience: a revised perspective', in McQuail, D. (ed.), *Sociology of Mass Communications,* Penguin, London, 1972.

McQuail, D., 'Alternative models of television influence', in Brown, R. (ed.), *Children and Television,* Collier Macmillan, London; Sage Publications Inc., USA, 1976.

HMSO, *Broadcasting,* London, 1966.

HMSO, *Report of the Committee on Broadcasting Coverage,* London, 1974.

HMSO, *Report of the Committee on the Future of Broadcasting,* London, 1977.

HMSO, *Royal Commission on the Press, Final Report,* London, 1977.

Rosengren, K.E. and Windahl, S., 'Mass media consumption as a functional alternative', in McQuail, D. (ed.), *Sociology of Mass Communications,* Penguin, London, 1972.

Vonnegut, Jr., K., 'Address to the National Institute of Arts and Letters', in Vonnegut Jr., K., *Wampeters, Foma and Granfalloons,* Delta, USA, 1971.

Index

References from Notes indicated by 'n' after page reference